sales@revenant.press
https://revenant.press/

The characters and events portrayed in this book are fictitious. Any similarity to real persons, living or dead, is purely coincidental and not intended by the author.

Revenant Press and the R Logo are Trademarks of Protos, LLC
Quantity sales. Special discounts are available on quantity purchases by corporations, associations, and others. For details, contact the publisher at the address above.

Editorial Services by Heather Monson.
Cover by Gary Wilkerson.

Gillespie, Brandon.
Activator: Success in the Tech Industry with Design Thinking / Brandon Gillespie.
First Printing, First Edition, February 2017

Contents

PREFACE

"There is nothing noble in being superior to your fellow man; true nobility is being superior to your former self."

- Ernest Hemingway

I have heard from many readers asking if I worked at the same places they do, because the stories shown herein seem so familiar. The reason is because we all often repeat similar patterns.

Ultimately, this book is about change. But change can only happen within, so this book is ultimately about changing ourselves, not others. James Allen, a western philosopher, aptly described this process by stating, "you will become as small as your controlling desire; as great as you dominant aspiration."

I challenge you to consider yourself carefully as you read this book. The last thing any of us wishes to do is admit to having fear, but this is the start of recognizing how we can change ourselves. Acknowledging the fear we each hold is the first step leading to self improvement. It is a choice we must make internally, by recognizing what is inside us that can use improvement, and then focusing upon making it better.

These challenges are things that come at us every day, and frankly we never do fully overcome them. But as we aspire to do better each day, we do improve, if only slightly. I often have to refer back to the principles described herein to remind myself of their importance. Something in our natures drives us to forget what elevates us, and leads us into baser habits.

I hope others find these principles as valuable as I have found them in my career.

THE PROBLEM

❝ *We cannot solve our problems with the same thinking we used when we created them.*

– Albert Einstein

If you were to ask someone in IT to build a house, they likely would start with the second-floor bathroom, regardless of the fact that there is no first floor. We have developed a curious ability to find something interesting in a project and to focus on it first, without necessarily considering the context of everything else that is needed for complete success.

This is compounded by how quickly technology changes, meaning many projects are left unfinished.

Consider a world where people move into houses still under construction, at least half of which are never finished, and when one actually is, we soon tear it down.

This is Information Technology (IT).

Before we can discuss how to improve, lets review some of the unique challenges we face.

Rapid Technology Innovation

The high rate of change sets the technology industry apart from all others. What is new today is old hat in a matter of years. This is true with consumer devices, as well as the expensive enterprise systems that drive the backbone of the world's computing systems. Multi-million dollar investments are made each year, with an expected lifespan of three to five years. How different would things be if we did the same with our houses—expecting to get the full value within a few years, after which we tore it to the ground and found a replacement.

I know of no other industry where a major investment is discarded and replaced so quickly. We tolerate this because the needs being met by the new technology are so valuable that they become critical to our plans, sometimes before they are even implemented. The technology that makes it into common use, however fractional, is often already obsolete, sometimes at just the point when we finally understand how to use it best. With such short life cycles, this dilemma has become perpetual.

Should we discard a partial investment and go to something new, or continue to hack away at something we know is already halfway into its grave?

A great example of this is server automation and the emerging world of containers. The industry just came to grips with how to automate and manage servers—or to use a car analogy: a robotic repair shop, making it easier and cheaper to do maintenance and updates. But just as this technology is coming into its own, along come containers. These are encapsulated vehicles that can be created easily, with little effort, and since they are so easy to create, there is no reason to maintain them — simply discard when finished. Suddenly, the investment in server automation seems wasted. People who spent years learning the inner workings of these automation frameworks (Puppet, Salt, Ansible, Chef, etc.) are now trying to figure out how to leverage these frameworks in containers—when the simple answer is don't! The world has changed, at just the point when it seemed to stabilize.

This rate of change creates an atmosphere of severe anxiety for anyone willing to admit it: How is it possible to understand the new technology, when it grows in complexity with every iteration, and each new release means everything we used to know is rendered useless? Because of this, it has become acceptable to ignore the big picture in order to cope with the immediate challenge. We just pick smaller pieces that make sense to us, and we focus on those fractions, while telling ourselves we are helping our customer.

The customer needs a second floor bathroom, right? Pay no mind to the missing first floor.

This environment of rapid technology change has fostered an attitude that partial success is okay. Within an organization, projects frequently spin up in competition with each other, only to be shut down and discarded before completion.

Simply put, the complexity of the industry multiplies so fast that we fear being able to understand everything, so we focus on the parts we know or can understand, just to keep sane—but this makes it difficult for us to design a truly strategic solution to meet our needs.

The rapid rate of technology change creates an almost-impossible task, and the innate fear that we each have around what we know and understand becomes a subtext to our entire approach.

Fear comes from so much more than the rate of change in technology. As a species, we are driven by our fears. Feelings deeper than thoughts motivate most of our actions, such as: am I able to provide for my family? Can I pay rent this month? How can I protect my children? Am I appreciated? What if I screw up? Did I hurt his feelings?

We fear that the little knowledge we do hold is suddenly obsolete, meaning we are no longer valuable to our organization. These fears bind us and drive every bit of our behavior.

Some cope with this by either focusing on specific technology disciplines (silos of knowledge), where others give up and join management, deferring the fear to other people. Whatever the reason, it is a fear of becoming obsolete, and in IT this obsolescence is calculated as a matter of a few years.

Within IT, fear has quietly and insidiously woven its way throughout the very fabric of how we do business. Success is no longer delivering a completed product across the finish line—instead, the rules are twisted, and it is about how many parts of the product we can finish before the technology is obsolete, the project is cancelled, or our funding is cut. Our very goals are now driven by failure, rather than success.

Recognizing this fear is important in understanding the 'what' and 'why' behind how IT is different from most other industries.

Technology Crusades

It seems that, just as we come to understand a new technology, it changes or becomes obsolete. It is no wonder that we develop emotional attachments to our solutions. The struggle to reach comprehension and understanding of a technology before it is obsolete is taxing and represents a notable accomplishment. This emotional bond to 'our' technology or methodology can become a passion that is almost religious—at least in how much we resist when somebody suggests a change, or in essence asks us to convert to a new religion we know nothing about.

When viewed through this perspective, the technology world becomes a vast tapestry of medieval dogma. Technologies, hardware, software, methodologies, and even specific ways of implementing hardware and software become the doctrines of these sects, and the practitioners—those people in the IT industry—become crusaders trying for the aggressive conversion.

Recognizing and understanding how people can become attached to technology and will fight for or against it with the vehemence of a 12th-century crusader is key to being able to maintain objectivity. Statistics, experts, and standards are rallied by these crusaders to match any technical argument. Just look hard enough—the internet is ripe with a variety of opinions backed by a little bit of truth. Any number of blogs can be harvested, and most vendors have a library of such scripture, or apocryphal texts on their competitors called "kill sheets."

While this sort of analogy seems a bit light-hearted, it is a very solid way of explaining the emotions and mind-sets we can slip into, if we are not careful.

For instance, if you have one server administrator who prefers brand-A of hardware, and another who prefers brand-B, be prepared for a battle when you have to purchase new hardware. Each administrator will present a laundry list of reasons to purchase one platform over the other, backed up with case studies, kill sheets, and market research to prove their case. The decision maker is usually left standing in the middle, feeling torn between two people.

The emotion we put into our technology decisions is difficult to overcome, because it is based in fear. We know how much effort we spent selecting the technology we like. We know how well it works for us. If we discard what we worked on, then we wasted our time and the company's, and consequently, if we wasted the company's time—is our job necessary?

It may not be logical, but these emotions are there, nonetheless.

Relationships and Conflict

I once worked at a corporation with Ray, a Sales Manager very frustrated with the IT department. He had certain needs, and they were not being met. For over a year, he had tried to get a solution to help his marketing team. However, the IT department had to balance the needs of the entire organization. There were many projects at play, as well as limitations in budget, and to do what he wanted just didn't fit well with the overall needs of the company.

Ray found a software solution that would ultimately make his team more effective and save on his budget, yet the IT department didn't appear interested. After months of trying to convince IT to purchase and install the software, he paid the $50,000.00 purchase price on his company credit card and asked one of his own people to install the software on a local workstation.

This action was, of course, met with scorn and anger from the propriety police within the department, with assertions and claims that he would get no support from IT. They branded Ray as being part of the "Shadow IT" and shunned his efforts within the organization.

But nobody asked the real question: what had we done to drive him to that point?

In this very real account, we were so blinded by our own fears of trying to meet all of the needs for the entire organization, while wrestling with constantly changing technology, that we forgot to empathize with his needs as a stakeholder. Technology, and the cycle of fear it brings, stood in the way, and we treated him like a cog in the machine.

Any time a customer is driven to find a solution outside of the normal channels, it is likely a signal that something is not working right.

Fear drives conflict and corrodes relationships.

Conversational Dissonance

Language is a poor and inefficient means of conveying ideas. This is evident by the fact that we keep changing our language, regardless of which one we use. Something written a hundred years ago is difficult for a modern reader to understand, because the language has changed in small but subtle ways. This is part of the ongoing evolution of our language, which happens as we struggle to better communicate.

Couple this with the imperfect nature of word definitions. We think we know what a word means, based on a dictionary reference, but in reality we have our own personal definitions of words, based on our past experiences of how that word is used. Our understanding is in this context.

Combine these language challenges with the unique composition of people drawn to the IT industry, which attracts a greater than normal ratio of people who are very focused on details, semantics, and literal explanations. This isn't a bad thing because people who think this way also tend to look at the world from a different angle and their mind is uniquely distinct from the neurotypical person—all in a manner that works well with technology. This alternate perspective helps them to make leaps of logic that they don't necessarily understand immediately, but with some analysis, are often found to be a good route forward.

However, along with this comes the fact that these technology mavens think and speak in a manner apart from most people. They tend to socialize like somebody who has learned a foreign language and may struggle to communicate subtle meanings. Through this, they may accidentally send the wrong signal, without even realizing it. Obsession with facts, an overly pedantic desire for literal statements, and confusion when people are offended when there was no intent to offend are common traits when these individuals are concerned. Recognizing if you have a different understanding of a word in these conversations can be a valuable tool to overcoming frustration on both party's account.

---

66 *Enterprise is like the ship in startrek...*

For example, the word 'enterprise' is frequently used in the IT industry. But have you ever paused to consider what it really means? What really differentiates 'Enterprise Technology' from regular technology? The meaning of the word enterprise, as it is defined in the dictionary, is simply: ingenuity, or boldness of energy. So how is Enterprise Technology different?

I had a conversation with a co-worker Gerry about a new project, at which time it came to light that our understanding of project scope differed dramatically, all based on the simple word, 'enterprise.' When we launched the project, our CIO had stated that the project was to provide an enterprise solution. My understanding of this statement came from the information I gave him, which was the software would integrate well with the other pillar systems in our environment, and it would lay the foundation for our strategy going forward. But I also knew it was a short-term solution. I had presented it to him as a bridge effort, with a short lifetime of two years, while we waited for the industry to mature. Therefore, common practices that would normally be employed around sustaining and operating the product could be reduced, such as having only two lanes for testing and development, instead of the organization's conventional three or four; and the solution didn't need costly Business Continuance features.

The disconnect in understanding emerged when Gerry explained that, to him, enterprise is like the ship in Star Trek. It was the pinnacle of technology, the flagship, and it had every single feature, bell, and whistle, which meant it should have Business Continuance and as many lanes as were needed. This was a very different understanding from my own, and all because of a single word that isn't even technical at its roots.

Entering into this language challenge comes the concept of a 'technical debate.' The entire thought of having a technical debate has become something to dread, even between people who enjoy technology. The rate of change drives so much new information, it is almost a guarantee that somebody will use a term or acronym that other people in the conversation do not understand. Most people recognize they cannot understand the technology, and they defer to the expert and just try to stay out of the way when the conversation shifts to something technical—for fear they will not know how to climb out of the morass of acronyms, jargon, and technical dialog that is flung about.

But this is elevated to an entirely new level when opposing crusaders argue their case about whose technology is better. Based in their own fears, they need to establish that everything they have learned is worthwhile—that they are useful. Therefore, when the case is argued, the conversation often involves technical 'babble'. This 'speaking in tongues' may be polite, but it is as vicious as any crusader meeting on the battlefield. It is a neanderthal ritual of chest thumping by adding more and more acronyms and obscure references to the conversation until one of the two contestants relents, backing away to lick their figurative wounds while leaving the other as the victor.

These patterns of failed communication are all a part of the Conversational Dissonance that often exists in IT. An example of how easy it is to stumble into this dissonance came about when I worked on a team that used several productivity tools. I used a popular graphics design tool to create diagrams and documentation for the project effort. Martin, the project manager, brought his tool to the team for task management, but it could also do diagrams and manage code—although we were not using these additional features.

One day, Martin stepped into my office with furled eyebrows and a glower cold enough to frighten small children, declaring that we must use his tool, and we must stop fighting against it. I was surprised, because I was already using his tool for task management. I thought he was suggesting we should use it for all of its remaining features, which he had suggested at previous times. I was unaware that he was frustrated with other team members, having just returned from a meeting with the developers, who were resisting using his tool for task management. He was just seeking an ally (Reference: *Dangerous Allies*).

From my perspective, this was an unplanned change that would create a significant work disruption, and the alarm it brought to me was high. Was it Martin's place to mandate, without any conversation, such a dramatic change to the very operational baseline of the team? It took a few days for us to recognize that what he stated was not what he intended to communicate.

He just wanted the entire team to use his tool for managing their tasks, not the entire scope of what it could do, and he was frustrated because some people on the team were not fully embracing it for task management. Martin took my surprise and defensive reaction as a signal that I must be one of the malcontents, and reacted in offense, even though in reality, there was no reason for contention because I didn't comprehend what he was trying to communicate.

In the face of the techno babble and literal statements, it can become easy to miss the fact that commonplace terms may also be disconnected, such as Enterprise. What one person defines as engineering may be another person's architecture.

The technical jargon, acronyms, obsession over details, and desire for clear literal statements creates a common condition found in IT, which is Conversational Dissonance. This dissonance can breed an air of frustration among customers, engineers, project managers, and leadership, if not properly understood and recognized.

Spending a moment with the entire team to discuss the culture of words to be used and what each of those words mean—the nomenclature of the project—is a worthwhile endeavor.

Change

There are many languages in common parlance around the world today. Yet some of these languages are considered dead, even though they are spoken daily, such as Gaelic and Latin. If it isn't usage, then what makes a language dead?

When it stops changing.

Consider how difficult it is to communicate ideas and thoughts to each other. This difficulty drives our language to change and evolve constantly. It is fascinating that the very definition of a living or dead language is based on when we stop trying to use it for important conversation. For what else is greater than the struggle of conveying our important knowledge between each other?

Everybody fears change. We like things to stay the same. It brings us comfort. Yet nothing improves without change.

Even if it is just turnover of the cells that make our bodies, change is a constant part of being alive—if we don't change, we are in a state of death.

This frightening statement explains how important change is to everything we do and how fear and change are critical elements that underlay all of our living activities—even more so in technology where the rate of change is so significant.

Time

Language and communication happen at fixed points in time. We have a thought, and a statement is made. Unlike a word processor, there is no undo feature. Time moves forward, and that statement you made or question you answered is now in the past. This creates a challenge to us, in that our communication is always framed on the stage of how much of the future we are willing to speculate about.

We constantly face a cognitive challenge where we live in the moment, yet the moment is fleeting. Our fears stop us from speculating too much about the uncertain future, but it is almost mandatory to think of it, just a little.

When the question is posed, "what are you doing for lunch?" We typically think of the most immediate time frame—our next lunch, even if it is currently 6:00 am. This is an example of us opening that perspective from the current moment into speculation of the future. The literal definition of the statement would be "what are you doing for lunch, right this moment," and if it was 6:00 am the correct answer would be "nothing."

Yet we don't think of it that way, we stretch our mind's eye forward to the future, consider possibilities, squelch fears and uncertainties we cannot control, and we offer a speculation framed like a fact, "I'm grabbing a sandwich." Even though other things may come into play by the time lunch arrives—the sandwich shop may close, or somebody may offer to take us to lunch elsewhere. Our understanding of the statement of future speculation is relaxed to allow for the flexibility of change, even though the words are exact.

This perspective of time is important to understand, as it is an important facet of technology conversations and strategic planning. Ironically, in our everyday lives we relax the future speculation without much concern, such as talking about lunch. Regardless of what we do, we frame our perspective of time as a window to the future, and this helps us to be able to communicate. The size of this window is relative to the distance forward in time we allow into our cognitive perspective.

Different people approach this in a wide variety of ways, especially when it comes to technology and the baggage of fear and change that comes along with it. With technology, we tend to be less flexible about this window, which can be fixed on a specific time frame, depending upon our job. Some people like to keep their window tightly focused and only worry about the next few weeks or months. Others have thrown their window wide open, and they bounce back and forth, sometimes within the same conversation, talking about something which is years away, then talking about something which is immediate.

I once entered into a presentation with a new customer where I was under the impression everybody knew we were talking about strategic future plans—a few years away. But we did not establish the time frame or window of time we were considering before beginning. During the conversation a statement was made about retiring some technology, and while nobody in the meeting spoke a word of complaint, afterwards the flames were stoked high.

The expectation of this window of time across years was that there would be plenty of time to research the situation and make an amenable solution to any challenge that could arise.

But the technology owners—those crusaders who loved their technology—lived in the world of support and maintenance. They had no need for a window of time beyond a few months, which would get them through the next patch and maintenance cycle and keep their customers happy.

So when they heard the statement that we would be replacing their technology, they immediately framed it in their own context—and heard that we would be replacing their technology in the next few months.

Immediately the sirens went off in their heads. Their fears and anxieties shifted into overdrive. They had personally invested years into building the system to be replaced. They knew it was highly unlikely anybody could replace something that took them years to build in so short a period of time.

What about the existing customers who were getting value out of the system, and would have nothing after it was shut down? Either we were idiots for making the proposal, or worse they were the idiots for having spent so much time on something which is obviously easier for somebody else to do.

The message went up the leadership channel that we didn't know what we were talking about, and it was ridiculous to think that we could succeed—the alternative in their perspective was not something to contemplate, as it struck at their ego and stoked their fears.

The missed context of time should have explained our proposal was a multi-year effort which would engage and involve the very individuals upset by the prospect—they were the ones who would be invested in making the technology decisions. Instead, they made assumptions based on poor communication, and these led to conflict that didn't need to exist.

It is when we forget to address the perspective of time, to empathize with our audience and learn what their perspective is, that we create problems in communication and in our relationships. Time is a factor to all things.

Understanding the context of time brought by each member of the audience helps maintain stable and healthy relationships.

Parataxic Distortion

Just like we each hold a window of time for our mind's eye, we also have a personal perspective, colored by our past experiences. These experiences, regardless of who shared them, change the assumptions we make about people's statements and actions.

Have you ever been in a situation where somebody assumed something about you and made a completely erroneous snap judgment? This view of the world, where each of us judges other people's actions and statements based on our own personal experiences and fears, is Parataxic Distortion.

We all do it.

Once, I had an open position for a Unix engineer. Vance, a Windows administrator from within the organization, with whom I had interfaced occasionally, applied for the position. All of my experiences with him were around Microsoft Windows. I knew he was a smart guy, enough to get into powershell and .NET programming.

At the time of writing this book, the industry has changed. However, at this time, Windows was in the spotlight, spreading everywhere. I knew of Unix engineers who were generally willing to do windows administration, but most of the Windows administrators would refuse to learn how to bring up a shell on a unix server, let alone try to figure out what seemed to be a labyrinth of commands and syntaxes, just to be able to get anything done.

I brought these past experiences to the situation. Stereotyping is something we do every moment of the day. It is required for us to be able to process the level of information that comes into us. But it can also get us into trouble when left unchecked, as it can lead to Parataxic Distortion.

In this situation, I read the resume and saw nothing on it that would indicate Vance was interested in working in the Unix world—thus, I wasn't interested in him as a candidate. My fear was that he would not be interested in the Unix world, where we desperately needed help, and may instead come at things with a Windows hammer, and this would cause friction with the other Unix administrators. However, there were others who thought he may be able to work out, and they asked me to interview him anyway.

I decided to challenge Vance to see if I could dig into his interests a little by poking at common fears, and I asked him if he would be comfortable running his primary desktop as Linux, not Windows. This was an exception to policy allowed only to few of the administrators in our organization. His answer was not just that he was willing, but he actually was hoping to do so, because he wanted to dive into the deep end and learn as much about it as he could. He got the job. He is a great administrator who provided great value, and I nearly passed him by.

This distortion can color more than just major moments and conversations—it can change our dialog. It is a challenge to recognize the distortion within ourselves, especially when we have allowed our own fears to reign. Being able to mentally step back, find your own fault in the scenario, and make corrections is vital to success.

WHAT IS DESIGN?

> *Design is how it works.*
>
> – Steve Jobs

Design is about understanding all relevant needs, in concert – both your customer's and your own. It brings all elements together in harmony. How do the needs interrelate with one another? How do you provide the most effective solution to those needs? This is design.

Design is important in technology because the rate of change creates anxiety and urgency. It becomes easy to take shortcuts to meet an immediate and pressing need, but if you have not taken the time to consider all needs in concert, you create a future burden that someday you will have to address. In IT this is known as Technical Debt.

As an example, early in the development cycle of a product I worked on, the development team selected an up-and-coming database engine, because it was getting good press, and it was something fun to play with. They did not consider the operational impact or customer needs. When it came time to bring the product to general release, the database struggled operationally—it could not scale, and it was not able to backup and replicate in the manner the customers required. This created a barrier to entry, and the cost to overcome it by switching out the database engine was greater than simply having spent the time up front to properly design the solution.

Often, design is framed as a process for problem solving—and when considered simply, this may be the case. However, effective design is not about solving problems. It is about solving needs. When we solve a problem, we focus upon the specific challenge before us, and we can miss the big picture. When approached this way, the problem takes the spotlight. Focusing on the problem typically leads us down a path of organic fixes and bolt-on repairs, instead of finding simple and efficient solutions that help our customer. The purpose of design is to spend time to understanding your needs so you can then make an educated decision.

Design Thinking is a mode of thought that helps use design principles in our daily work, so we solve for a need, rather than solving a problem. It encourages thinking outside of the box by seeking an improved future state. Design Thinking can involve problem resolution, but it is not about simply fixing problems. It is a different approach to help you integrate design into your work, whether dealing with complex multidimensional issues, or completing basic daily tasks.

To avoid confusion, within the Technology Industry there are two disciplines that both use design: Architects, and Designers. Architects are focused on the technical and scientific design challenges, while Designers are focused on the aesthetic and usability design challenges. Throughout this book the term design applies equally to both.

What is an Architect?

Technology Architects and Strategic Planners may be the most confused roles in the IT industry. Depending upon whom you ask or where you look, the definition varies dramatically.

While the industry has struggled with defining the role of an Architect, an alternate label has also come into common use, which is the Strategic Planner. Of course, this also is poorly defined. From my perspective, an effective Information Technology Architect and a Strategic Planner both fill the same role. For the sake of simplifying the conversation, I will use the term Architect.

Some common perceptions of an Architect are:

- A lead developer or engineer.
- Somebody who understands the overall technology systems and knows where each part fits.
- Somebody who designs software systems and can program well.
- Somebody who wrestles with the challenges of how a system works and designs a usable system.
- Somebody who changes technology, or an "agent of change."
- Somebody who dictates technology standards, but often without understanding the needs.
- Somebody who designs a new technology infrastructure or software implementation for a business.
- Somebody who is difficult to work with.

31

None of these roles directly addresses relationships and mitigating fear in relationships. In many cases, the relationship with an Architect is considered in the negative context—that they are difficult to work with.

Because of the fear everybody holds about the rate of change for technology, we all want to have somebody else worry about the big picture. But at the same time, we want to control the smaller part that affects us, without somebody else meddling in it. This is a catch-22 scenario and is likely why the role of Architect is so confused. We understand the need for somebody else to recognize the big picture, but we aren't comfortable with defining what an Architect should do, besides just knowing the big picture.

An Architect is commonly perceived as a gatekeeper in this scenario. The dialog usually goes something like, "I want to do this thing, may I please do it?" and then cringing while waiting for a declarative reason the wanted feature will not work, or even a lengthy dissertation on how it flies in the face of everything ever considered for future strategies.

The question posed above defines the conventional Authoritarian role people consider an Architect to hold, and they resent it. This relationship is much more effective if the aspect of Design Thinking and planning is brought into the mix. An Architect placed in an organization with an Authoritative position instead of Authoritarian, along with the proper tools, can change the question in a beneficial manner. The simple way to keep these two concepts separate is to consider the word sounds themselves: Authoritative works in a consultative fashion, where Authoritarian tends to tear apart relationships.

The difference between the two is important, and it centers around fear and change. An Authoritarian role comes with force and inflexibility, where an Authoritative role is consultative and guiding. An Authoritative role creates a healthy relationship with each member of a team. Authoritative recognizes and understands the boundaries (strategies), but also recognizes that exigent circumstances come up and is willing to work out variances to facilitate progress.

In this context, the question posed above can be rephrased as, "I want to do this thing. Do you see any problems with it? And if so, can you help me work out a remediation effort?"

Considering these things, the role of an Effective Architect (Authoritative) can be described by four key elements:

- **Relationships** – The ability to empathize with both technical and non-technical audiences, understand their needs and fears, and be able to communicate with all in a language they understand.
- **Analysis** – The ability to decompose complex systems into digestible elements, and the capability of understanding the technological relationships among different needs.
- **Planning** – The ability to understand the business's core needs, industry direction, partner road maps, and how to bring these together in concert to provide an effective solution.

- **Execution** – The ability to enact plans. What role does an Architect take during the different execution and control phases of a project?

A final consideration on Architects in an organization is the degree of technology ownership they hold. If they are the ultimate decision maker, it is more likely that they will slip into an Authoritarian role. However, if they exist in a role that empowers them to be a valuable reference asset, this enables them to be Authoritative.

Design Deliverables

Everything is about deliverables—or the product of our work effort. Yet, when we are involved in a design cycle, what should be the product of design is often overlooked. If design deliverables in your organization are not clearly defined, then the role itself is also not well understood. Yet it is very common to find people with the role of Architect who have vaguely defined deliverables who are not empowered to engage with the technology owners. This is not only a waste of organization resources, but also frustrating for all parties involved. The Architect will find they have no real influence, and those they interface with will find their involvement a distraction. Some organizations have gone so far as to intentionally setup Architects in this manner, because the organization is paralyzed with a fear of conflict, yet still recognizes the need of an Architect.

Breaking through this barrier can be as simple as defining and authorizing Design deliverables. At the highest level, there are three key products:

- **Tactical Plans** – near-term how things are to be done (the tools and actions)
- **Strategic Plans** – long-term what needs are to be met (the needs and function not tools)
- **Variances** – process and documentation to manage variances from the plans

An important facet of both the Tactical and Strategic plans is to include a Total Cost to Own analysis, discussed later.

Variances can be the most important deliverable as far as relationships are concerned. They are how you deal with the inevitable need for change that arise and they help to recognize that time is fluid. Having a clearly understood variance process is critical to maintaining friendly and strong relationships, both internally and externally. How will these changes be handled and incorporated into the ongoing effort? This is a defined process for empathizing with the changing needs of a customer, identifying tactical variances, and putting in place either a 'get well plan' to bring the resulting deliverable inline with the strategic baseline, or adjusting the strategic baseline to incorporate the new deliverable.

The *Strategic Plan* is what people conventionally consider Architecture, and it should factor many of the elements described in this book, including different contexts of time (the further out it describes things, the more it should focus on function over tools).

The *Tactical Plan* is split into three views, which are based on the audiences. Having documents for each of these views helps to reduce the complexity of each. When attempts are made to cover the needs described in these three views as a single document, the single document usually becomes overly complex and difficult to understand. These views are:

- **Structural** – high level overview of components and relationships
- **Behavioral** – the way data flows
- **Execution** – the way a system is constructed.

The *Structural* documentation describes the parts of a system and the relationships of each part. This is targeted to systems administrators (or devops engineers) so they can understand the underlying details. This could be a detailed view of servers, networking, software stacks, and other components that makeup the whole solution and how they relate to each other. In many cases, the Structural view may also need to be layered in levels of detail, depending upon the complexity of the system. See *Appendix-1: Structural Document*, for an example.

A *Behavioral* document describes the way data is managed and flows in the system. Structural elements are usually abstracted into behavioral roles, without the technical minutia. The purpose of a Behavioral document is to help future developers and systems engineers be able to integrate with systems as well as to help debug problems that arise in data movement. The focus is upon how data moves, transforms, and is used within the system. While at a structural level a server cluster may be explained in detail, in the Behavioral view, it is only described by its purpose (an application) and shows how the data moves between the different applications. See *Appendix-2: Behavioral Document*, for an example.

The *Execution* document describes the construction or implementation of a system. Processes, scripts, testing, automation and other systems are described at this level. This is most often forgotten. It should be possible to rebuild a system with nothing more than the Execution documentation. Reference *Documentation Driven Change (DDC)* for a useful tool to help facilitate good Execution documentation using Agile implementation methodology. Execution documentation is used by those who support a system to know how it was built, avoid tribal knowledge, and be able to make future changes more easily.

Generally speaking, these products should come as iterative steps during the Design Thinking process. When working on the *Empathy* phase, the Structural design can be fleshed out as the needs are better understood, along with some skeleton work for the Behavioral document. During the *Creativity* phase these are further referenced as different prototypes are evaluated, and before *Rationality* the Structural and Behavioral documents should have some concrete details, at least to the general level, while the Execution document can be completed during *Execution*. Finally, all three documents should be reviewed and reconciled during the last phase of *Rationality: Learn*.

DOCUMENTATION DRIVEN CHANGE

A monumental task in the technology industry is building useful execution documentation. It is such a challenge that most teams do not even do it, or if it does exist, it is a pale shadow of what is actually implemented. This becomes a great challenge when bringing new staff on board, transitioning work efforts between teams and team members, or dealing with a disaster recovery scenario.

Most engineering efforts actually work in an iterative 'agile' manner, even if they are not managed as an Agile project. This is because the most common approach in engineering and 'figuring out' a solution is to do so by trial and error, not by referencing pre-made blueprints that describe how to do everything. When implementation happens in this manner, the last thing somebody wants to do after wrestling through hours of work is to go back and write down how it was done; and frankly speaking, many of the steps taken to get to completion are likely forgotten. If the Execution document happens at all, it is commonly an afterthought, and much of the requisite fidelity of detail is lost in the rear-view mirror of the situation.

Documentation Driven Change (DDC) is a simple and effective way to create good Execution documentation in an Agile world. DDC is not implementing a formal Change Control process. DDC documentation could be used in a Change Process, but that is beside the immediate point, which is to get useful Execution Documentation. To add further complexity, with server and configuration automation documenting change becomes even more curious because much of the final product is declarations and configurations in a system. However, DDC can be the driving force behind exploration efforts, and the resulting document can become a basis for new automation.

DDC follows in the footsteps of software development's Test Driven Development (TDD), where the desired result must first be described with a test, then the software is written to match the test. With DDC, a document begins by describing the expected outcome, and is then expanded with the explicit code, steps, commands, and actions to bring the change to fruition. Ideally, the commands are typed into the document first, and then cut-and-pasted into the actual system where the change is happening. The resulting document may look very similar to the popular "How To" blogs that walk somebody through doing a few simple steps. While this may seem like simple logic, the pragmatic reader will know it is opposite of how most IT implementations work, despite what processes may exist.

For example, an administrator is tasked in figuring out how to do hot backups for a new MariaDB server. Using DDC, the administrator opens a working document and labels it for the specific action "MariaDB Hot Backups." Then, as they research and learn information, they paste into this document the steps they want to first try.

These might be:

1. Setup backup space for hot backups. (Include a link to the "Adding Backup Disk document")

```
cd /repo/base/path
curl -kO https://remote.host/version.12.rpm
createrepo .
```

2. Download latest copy of hot-backup software into org system repository, such as

```
dnf -y install hot-backup-software
```

3. On destination server, install hot-backup software from org repository:

And so forth. Then, the administrator attempts to execute on their own drafted plan. This usually is met with some things not working as expected, and the documentation is updated before the next iteration, becoming more and more refined until it represents the final product.

The key to DDC is to keep the documentation as lightweight as possible, both in creation and sustainability. Setting up screen shots is less desirable than simply referencing the steps that should be taken, such as:

• Select the File Men->Open and check [New Tasks]

The DDC document should not necessarily be an authoritative source. In the world of highly advanced system automation, DDC can simply be the first step to making an automation service.

Good DDC documentation has a few elements:

1. Replay Ability: It can be handed to somebody else with an equal level of technical aptitude as the original author, and that second individual can reproduce the results.
2. Simple: if the execution document is littered with too much information and pages of screenshots, it is probably too difficult to sustain, let alone easily read and follow.
3. Cut-and-Paste: blocks of control commands are identified easily, and formatted so they can be cut-and-pasted.
   - Do not include prompts (i.e. `$ command` is less useful than simply `command`).
   - CLI interfaces are easier to document and replay than GUI.
4. When referencing a GUI, keep it simple. Describe the GUI action, rather than using screenshots:
   - Select the *File Menu*, then *Open->Task List* and check *New Tasks*

As with any tool, there is a right place and time. With automation services, the role of DDC becomes even more relevant. Simply saying "my documentation is my automation" is not valuable, as often times the automation is normalized and abstracted into a wide variety of templates and objects. This makes it very difficult for a person to read through the automation system to figure out how something works, unless they have a degree in technology archaeology. The DDC Execution Documentation, however, can be the first step that leads to automation, and it can be updated when major changes to the system are needed.

Design Thinking

There are three phases to Design Thinking: *Empathy, Creativity,* and *Rationality.* You start by *Empathizing* with the problem to find the needs, then move into *Creativity,* considering ideas and possible solutions, followed by *Rationality* in deciding and implementing the best path forward.

In order to use Design Thinking effectively, it is important to recognize which phase you are in, and focus on doing only the steps in that phase. If you are in the Empathy phase, you should be focused on finding the needs, not on the different ways you could fix the problem. If you are in the Creativity phase, you should have a grounded understanding of the issue to be solved and the identified needs of that issue, so you can better consider what solutions might be of use. And by the time you reach the Rationality phase, you should have already selected the powerful solution you want to implement.

As with all elements of design, flexibility in allowing movement back and forth between phases is important. Sometimes things change—you may discover knew information not previously known, priorities in your organization have moved, or perhaps the industry itself has shifted. Understanding the elements of each phase helps you to work with them in your daily life.

This book is a description of the process of Design Thinking, along with tools that can be used to help apply it in your daily lives. Because **Planning** is so much an integral part of what makes Design, it is discussed next, followed by the three phases of Design Thinking: **Empathy**, **Creativity** and **Rationality**. Afterwards we discuss the biggest challenge to implementations, which is **Preparing for Change**.

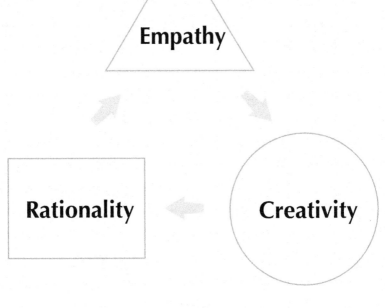

PLANNING

> *A goal without a plan is just a wish.*
>
> – Antoine de Saint-Exupéry

Whether you are working the design of a one-month effort or a five-year strategy, a plan is an extremely powerful tool that helps to defer personal fears and strengthen relationships. A plan is the calming salve that helps in the process of designed change.

How often have you been faced with a situation where different parts of an organization wish to do their own thing, instead of working together? I once asked Laine, a Director of R&D at a large software company, "What is the biggest challenge to your organization's success?" His answer was that the directors of the business units he supports, or his customers, continue to go out and make deals with outside vendors in matters that should involve him, yet they do it without his centralized organization being involved. Then they want him to support these deals, even though he wasn't part of the decision process. How can they really expect him to be engaged with something where he wasn't even part of the decision process? Both Laine and his customers are honest and good people. They are not trying to undermine each other. Yet, despite how much he tries, they persist in making their own arrangements.

I suspect the real reason is quite simple: he and his customers have not invested together in a unified strategic plan. Planning is the tool we use to calm our fears. When we prepare for a camping trip, it would be stressful to those joining us if we just randomly tossed a few items into the car and took a ride into the sunset, not even certain where we were going, let alone if we had even brought the right gear. We all like planning, to different degrees. Some of us like it more than others, and it is usually rooted in how much we dislike uncertainty.

" Competing plans lead us to conflict

When we see somebody doing something that isn't part of our plan, it causes us stress, and we start to think about how it is going to mess up our plans—basically, our fears kick in. But we should ask ourselves: why is it my plan vs theirs—what happened to our plan? Competing plans lead us to conflict, and they exist because we are not communicating properly.

I am certain we have all heard the adage, "your lack of planning doesn't constitute an emergency on my part." This is something often repeated when we are stressed because something is dumped into our lap.

The problem here is the statement is as far from the truth as it could possibly get. Of course it constitutes an emergency on your part, if you care about your relationships and your customers.

Planning is best performed as a partnership, not a solo activity. Being able to empathize with somebody's needs is being willing to help them plan. A proper plan has investment from all stakeholders. It has taken into account your customer's fears, as well as your own. The plan discusses a possible future state, it is flexible enough to handle change, and it is something all parties agree to. If people are making their own plans outside of the shared plan, they are likely not invested as a partner in the shared plan.

The importance is to have a plan, and to communicate the plan. In its absence our fears drive us to create our own plans, regardless of how ineffective they may be.

My grandfather served in the US Navy just after World War II. He was posted as an electronics technician on the bridge of a destroyer patrolling the Enewetak Atoll during nuclear bomb testing at the Marshall Islands. There was a plan and process explained to the crew. Most of the seamen were instructed to turn away at the signaled time, but some people—notably those on the bridge—were given welder's goggles to wear during the nuclear detonation.

This was the plan to keep them from being blinded. However, nobody knew what to expect, and fears abounded. The world was fascinated by the discovered power and destruction of the atom, and they knew well what sort of destruction this caused in Japan. Now they were ready to witness the next test. While his ship was miles from the detonation, he had the equivalent of front-row seats.

At the signaled time, the crew turned away or donned the goggles, and the bomb was detonated. He reported that it all happened rather quickly, just a brilliant flash of light brighter than anything he had ever seen before.

Then afterwards, once the all clear was given, the Lieutenant leaned to my grandfather and said, "I know we had the goggles, but I also closed one eye . . . just in case."

With the knowledge we have today this may seem like a frivolous action. But it demonstrates how any plan, regardless of how unfeasible it may be, helps to alleviate our fears—even in the most trying of situations. The Lieutenant didn't know if it would help or not, but he feared his eyes would burn out, and this drove him to decide his own supplementary plan and course of action in an attempt to alleviate the fear.

In reality, we care more about having *any* plan than we care if the plan succeeds. The absence of a plan is what creates fear, and its presence suppresses that fear. Our customers may trust our skills and experiences, but they still like the reassurance that we understand and empathize with their fears and needs, through the communication of a documented plan that they helped to build.

It is important to know that **Plans give Direction, Plans Change**, and the value of a **Strategic Plan**.

Plans give Direction

A plan's importance cannot be over-emphasized. One of the most relevant reasons for a plan is it gives us a direction. If we do not know where we want to be, we will never be able to get there.

Consider the situation of an 1800's farmer driving a horse and plow in his field. These fields were often hand-cleared, and objects too unwieldy to remove were left in place. As the farmer worked his way across the field, he would pick a fence post in the distance and drive towards it. When he encountered an obstacle such as a large boulder, he would work around the obstacle, then re-orient onto the fencepost and continue on his way without diverging too much from his original direction. The fence post allowed him to know where he was going. Without the fence post to show him his goal, each time he hit an obstacle, his direction could be dramatically altered.

A plan gives us the fence posts we need in our future, so people are able to stay on track as obstacles are encountered. That isn't to say that a plan will not change because of an obstacle, but it helps us to find our course again after we work around the obstacles.

Plans Change

*"A good solution applied with vigor now is better than a
perfect solution applied ten minutes later"*

– George S. Patton

It is important to understand that the same
challenge of time and the window of our mind's eye, as
discussed in *The Problem: Time*, also applies to our Plans.
The concept that we have to make a decision in the
moment about a future we simply cannot know wreaks
havoc with our assumptions, beliefs, and communications.
It can lead us to act too early, or to be paralyzed with
indecision and act too late.

We create a plan to help us alleviate our fears
about not knowing something. But at the same time,
changing a plan can cause the same fear, if not properly
communicated. Our customers may start to feel like we
don't know what we are doing, or that their opinion no
longer matters.

Whatever we plan now will change. The most
effective plans are fluid, not rigid. The information,
limitations, and environment known to us at the time a
plan is made will change. When these things change, the
plan may need to change as well.

Make certain to involve everybody in plan changes
to the same degree they were involved with the formation
of the plan, if not to a greater degree. This communication
will strengthen the relationship. Some project management

disciplines have this flexibility built into their process; others do not. It is useful in either scenario to document how you will handle changes to the plan.

Strategic Plans

"Good tactics can save even the worst strategy, bad tactics will destroy even the best strategy"

– George S. Patton

Strategy is about what you want to do, where Tactics are about how you will do it. Plans have both a Strategic and Tactical angle. How you do something is generally decided fairly near the time it is implemented, which means a Tactical plan is focused on the near term, where a Strategic plan covers the longer term things but stays out of the particulars of how it will be implemented. Successful Strategic plans focus on the needs (or what is being done) and avoid the actions (how it will be done).

The reason for this is time. When considering a plan, you can specify how something will happen, but when looking beyond a few months, specific actions and technological implementations become much harder to predict. Tactical planning focuses on the short term and is about specific implementation details such as the tools to be used, where Strategic planning is focused on years and is about needs being met.

Effective strategic plans understand the business needs, recognize how those needs are being met with current technology, and describe how to better meet those needs over time. The definition of *Needs* and the distinction of *Primitive Needs* are fully explored in *Phase 1 - Empathy: Relationships: Needs*.

The important takeaway is that Strategic plans should be aware of the timeframe, and should not linger on tools. A tool is not a need. Keeping focus on the needs orients our minds to think strategically, where getting too deep into the details can create a plan which is not flexible enough to adapt as your world changes. Though sometimes we cannot avoid including tools in the strategic plan, tools in IT inevitably will be different on something planned three years out. However, the need is not as likely to change. This focus on needs also helps to avoid the crusaders, who tend to instead think in terms of tools.

When considering needs for a Strategic Plan, facilitate your needs analysis by considering two questions:

- Where do my customers want to be?
- Where will the tools be?

A strategic plan becomes documentation for where an organization wants to go and how the technology will improve upon meeting the organization's direction over time. This is an iterative process that is revisited yearly, if not quarterly, through communications and relationship management.

To help understand effective strategic plans, lets contrast two different types, based on the various strategies I have seen presented around investing in cloud hosting technologies:

1. "We will migrate 50% of our services to cloud provider ABC within 2 years," and it then goes on to discuss costs of the ABC vendor at today's rates.
2. "Cloud Services enable us to lower the overall ownership costs of infrastructure and to empower our administrative staff to do more in helping the company with services the cloud providers are not offering, such as dev-ops automation and continuous integration." It goes on to describe the SaaS and PaaS offerings that are currently available in the market, and how they can be leveraged in contrast to the existing datacenter.

The first plan does not discuss the needs of the company, nor how any of the given services will address them. It just discusses a vendor (the tool) and even the prices at today's rates. But it is scoped in a strategic timeframe (2 years).

The second plan outlines the value of the cloud services and even identifies where the organization might be struggling (automation and continuous integration). It does not discuss which vendor should be used—just the that the merits can expand capabilities without having to increase internal service and datacenter costs. This second plan provides much greater value and is more attainable because it has spent time to identify the needs and discuss a plan for addressing those needs that doesn't discuss specifics around the 'how'. It may even provide an internal assessment for how much it would cost (in labor, infrastructure, and time) to build and provide the same services in its own datacenter, as a contrast to the external service.

When reviewing at a strategic plan, look to see if it discusses the hows—named tools and vendors. Whether it gets into these details or not can be used as a simple test to identify quality and value. Good plans avoid the tools and focus on the needs being addressed.

Strategic Planning fundamentally uses Design Thinking principles, and empowers an organization by providing a framework that helps to remind us how to think in a design oriented manner.

FRAMEWORKS AND METHODOLOGIES

There are numerous dissertations and explanations about Strategic Planning frameworks and methodologies for Enterprise Architecture. The purpose here is not to describe a framework or method—it is up to you to decide which framework is best for you, once you recognize that frameworks and methodologies are simply methods to help address fear responses. The purpose of this work is to explain the motivating factors behind the way people act in Information Technology and to explain how the elements of Design Thinking can be leveraged to address these human factors. Without understanding the motivations behind the behavior—the fears that exist in the system—and the basic principles of design, working to apply a framework is premature.

Further reading on frameworks, beyond the simple concepts of Design Thinking, can include the Zachman Framework, Enterprise Architecture Planning (EAP), Federated Enterprise Architecture (FEA), TOGAF, and DoDAF. Please investigate which framework, if any, fits best for your organization. The remainder of this book describes principles, behaviors, and tools applicable to all.

PHASE 1 – EMPATHY

> *When you show deep empathy toward others, their defensive energy goes down, and positive energy replaces it. That's when you can get more creative in solving problems.*
>
> – Stephen Covey

We cannot change what we do not understand; to properly address something, we must understand it at the most primitive level. The *Empathy* phase of Design Thinking is about finding a primitive level of understanding of the challenge so you can move into the *Creativity* phase with a true understanding of what you need to do. If working in the context of Project Management, Empathy should happen during project Initiation.

An important part of Empathy is recognizing the relationships in all things, and being able to properly analyze needs. To do this, we must better understand our teams, how we communicate in meetings, and what it means to have ownership and how Negativity can have a detrimental effect.

The *Empathy* phase of Design Thinking has two key steps: **Define** and **Research**. These steps can be worked in any order, and often are worked in parallel. During the Define step you identify the issue, audience, stakeholders, and what success looks like. For Research, you take time to fully understand the issue or problem you are faced with by looking at it from all possible angles.

Tools to help with Define and Research are described throughout the rest of this section, and at the end we will summarize the key elements of each step.

Relationships

Relationships are how two or more people, objects, or concepts are connected. But relationships are hard to understand because we spend most of our time focusing on the people, objects, problems, politics, or concepts, rather than the connection—the actual relationship. The difficulty is that a relationship is not tangible. It is not something we can see or touch—it is only something we can feel. It is the empathy and demands that exist between each party when we collaborate.

66 *Relationships are about what we leave behind*

More than anything else, however, relationships are about what we leave behind: the feelings, impressions, and thoughts that make up the history of who we are.

The importance of the actual relationship is surprising, yet so hard to grasp. In the world of story writing, much effort is spent in teaching new authors about character flaws, to the point that many burden their characters with so many physical and mental ailments that, if the characters lived in the real world, they would likely be debilitated to the point of total non-function. These authors have missed the point of a relationship. The flaws merely exist to define the challenges in the connection between two characters—or the relationship. But instead they focus on the flaws, not the connection.

What the writing instruction misses by its focus on characterization and flaws, is that it isn't the flaws that make a character, it is the relationships challenged by those flaws. The relationship is what makes it an interesting story to us, not the flaws. The simple way to identify a good story is to look at the relationships.

Consider a simple tale:

There was a young boy who walked along a creek, picked a flower, and took it home.

This is not interesting.   Perhaps instead:

Cole is a young boy with a tangle of dark hair. On this day he searches the creekside to find just the right flower. It is a special flower that his sister likes, and he knows this because before she was sick, the two would play at this creek and she would pluck the flower, sticking it in her hair while telling him stories about being a princess. He remembers her smiling a lot back then, and this doubles his concentration.

A splash of color catches his eye, and he see's the flower among the grass. His pulse quickens. He plucks the flower, and runs back to the house. His relatives are all visiting, and he has to sneak in the back door just so they won't send him away. They told him to stay away from his sister and let her rest.   But she is already sleeping all day!

As he sneaks into her quiet room, disturbed only by the beep of medical equipment. He remembers how much she liked the flower, how it brought a smile to her face, and he knows it will help.

She blinks at him in the dim light from the hallway, her head covered in a cap for the warmth. Then she see's the flower he placed on her pillow, and like warm glow of twilight, a smile brightens her face, trembling at first, but turning into a great grin as she wipes a tear from her eye.

That is a relationship.

Much like the boy in this story, a good relationship drives us to action and investment in the other party. We must act to satisfy the relationship—failing to maintain its health will not only damage the relationship, it will leave us empty.

Healthy relationships are two-way streets, in which everyone involved receives what they need, but this works only with empathy and service to each other. For the validation we may receive, our care, concern, and help to the other person gives them the same. With a good relationship, both parties are stronger with it than without it.

A good relationship cannot be one-way. If somebody doesn't care what the other person has to say or bring to the equation, then they are in a bad relationship. Consider this in the context of a common statement made about somebody resisting change, "If they will not accept the change, they can be reintroduced to the workforce." Is that a one-way relationship, or two-way?

When in conversations, we must listen with the intent to understand. If all we are doing is waiting for a moment to respond, we have failed.

Relationships are at the heart of any effort's success. No deliverable can be made without many people's involvement, and each person is a valuable member. Even the simplest relationship of a customer to an implementer has two actors. When that relationship is broken, nothing effective can be developed for the customer. Either the implementer will resent the work, or the customer will fail to trust in the result.

In the IT world, the people, objects, and concepts that compose the relationships can be grouped into four categories: **Customer, Implementer, Needs,** and **Constraints**. Customers have Constraints. Implementers have Needs. The Needs, themselves, may have Needs and Constraints. These all come together in creating a matrix of relationships, where each relationship among Customer, Implementer, Needs, and Constraints feature additional aspects of **Communication** and **The Power of Sustainment**.

These topics are now explored in depth.

CUSTOMER

Customers are anybody receiving the product or benefit of your effort. Customers can be external to your organization or internal. Without customers, there is no reason to do the work.

IMPLEMENTER

Implementers are those involved in creating the product for a customer. This includes the engineers, operators, developers, designers, and any other facilitator or individual part of the process, who is not a customer. As an added level of complexity, sometimes Implementer's can be customers to each other.

NEEDS

Needs are a key part of the matrix independent of the customer—this is what somebody wishes to have satisfied in a relationship. The inflection point between success or failure is based in the ability to understand the primitive needs on both sides of the relationship. The needs of a customer are equal to the needs of an implementer. Furthermore, the relationship of these needs and the constraints of the project are also needs that must be identified.

It is important to consider all needs together, not just one at a time. When we consider the needs together with their matrix of relationships to each other, we can find the most harmonious solution, and our velocity for delivery is increased. When we only focus on one need at a time, it may feel like we are working faster because we deliver quickly, but in reality our overall velocity is reduced because of rework. This creates what is called technical debt, or basically work you have deferred to the future, but which will have to be paid for at some point.

Consider a world where we didn't know what an automobile was, but a customer came to us with a need for a mode of transportation. As we analyze their need, we discover other needs: somewhere to sit on the vehicle, wheels, a frame, an engine, and a mechanism to steer the vehicle. If we just pick the first logical deliverable—wheels and a frame—we can be happy to build and deliver that to the customer. Progress!

Then we select the next item—something to steer the vehicle. In careful consideration, we decide the best place for the steering mechanism is at the front, before the axle and wheels. This puts the driver in a great position to see all things. We then build tie rods and the mechanism to make the wheels turn and deliver this to the customer. Even more progress!

Next, we have to figure out where to put the engine. But we find the best location for the engine is also in the front of the vehicle. Unfortunately, that is where we put the driver and steering system! To make this engine deliverable work, we have to tear out our previous effort and retool it, and our velocity is dramatically reduced. We unknowingly created technical debt by not looking at our overall needs.

If we had considered all needs up front, understanding how the needs depend upon each other and have their own inter-dependent relationships, we could have avoided this problem. Recognizing the relationships of the needs to themselves as well as the customer, and the most effective way to bring them together in concert, helps us avoid building organic Rube Goldberg solutions which are difficult to use, inefficient, and fail to provide great value to the customer.

When discussing needs with a customer, it is important to understand the differences among a need, a deliverable, and a feature. This is explored in detail in *Phase 1 – Empathy: Analysis: Decomposition*—at a simple level: A need is something that must happen, usually driven by fear, and can be phrased as a question (See: *The Critical Question*). A deliverable is a product or part of a product that is functional on its own and is provided to a customer to meet one of their needs. A feature is an aspect of a deliverable that cannot stand on its own as a functional unit for delivery. For example, a deliverable may be the steering mechanism for a vehicle. It could be put into any vehicle, thus it stands on its own. The turn radius supported by the steering mechanism becomes a feature of that deliverable.

CONSTRAINTS AND RISK

Constraints define the boundaries, limitations, and risks that limit our capability to deliver. This is very true when it comes to relationships. Going to a meeting with a customer and only discussing the great things to be accomplished 'someday' may seem fun, but none of it will come to fruition without also discussing potential pitfalls, roadblocks, and show stoppers.

We are defined by our constraints, not our capabilities, because these are what limit us—where our capability of improving should be unending. Avoid thinking of constraints as insurmountable roadblocks, but merely the available roads to travel. The key is to identify the potential constraints as early as possible in the planning phase, so you can adjust for them, rather than having them unexpectedly appear and cripple your effort in the middle of the project.

Yet we often fear constraints and risks, worry about them, and consider them as unreasonable demands placed by management. How often have we been in a situation where somebody came and asked for a deliverable with a frighteningly short period of execution time?

Our immediate thought may be defiance—the request is impossible. We don't understand the relationship demands which motivated the initial request, so this defiance is rooted in fear that our needs and our customers' needs will not be met.

However, constraints don't have to be detrimental. They can be powerful tools. I worked on a project for a military installation several years ago where a significant program for maintenance and repair on the next generation war machine would be granted to the base that could first build a datacenter to house its needs. This had a significant economic impact for the area, but it was a steep commitment.

Three bases were up for consideration. Leadership from each of the three bases discussed who could build the facility and how long it would take. Our leadership halved the estimate of the other two bases and were given a tentative go-ahead. Then they came to us and asked for the impossible. Could we build a datacenter, with all of the classified requirements, in a thirty-by-ninety foot storage area of a 1950's train depot, all in a matter of months?

Just negotiating a contract for drywall alone, in the military, would normally take the entire time for the estimated effort—daunting didn't begin to describe the magnitude. But the importance was conveyed as well, and we used principles of Design Thinking—empathy in relationships—and others of these principles to engage everybody, including the sub-sub-contractors, into our success. In a flurry of productivity, the room was designed, planned, rebuilt—with an unexpected asbestos abatement thrown into the mix (an unplanned risk). The facility was delivered on time, allowing for the granting of the program—a major win for the entire state.

When fear is properly managed, and people feel empathy from those with whom they interact, then everybody involved is elevated to a greater level of success. The challenge, however, is the ease at which we let our fears consume us.

THE POWER OF SUSTAINMENT

Perhaps it comes from my experience in working in the Department of Defense, but I have come to appreciate a simple facet of Relationships called Sustainment.

The concept is seemingly obvious, yet so often lost and forgotten. Simply put, one must always provide respect upwards to leadership, laterally to peers, and downwards to subordinates.

If you have ever been in the situation where somebody is presenting a topic or concept, and their supervisor (or perhaps even you) states something to the effect of, "I haven't approved this yet," then you have just witnessed a relationship withering because that manager did not provide sustainment.

It is okay to have a disagreement of opinion, but to contradict or act against another's influence, whether they are present or not, is the easiest way to lose respect—both with them to you, and with others.

The subtlety of Sustainment is hard to fully comprehend. It is in the small messages we send, perhaps even without intending to do so.

Once when I started with a new team, after coming directly from the consulting world where we provided weekly activity reports as part of our contract, I asked my team to provide similar reports to me. My fears were that I didn't know what the team was doing, and I could not correlate the team's actions to what the customers were saying about the team's results. I didn't want to be surprised with a claim from a customer about what somebody on the team was doing, and not be able to support the team properly.

However, the team did not like the idea of doing weekly reports. They had never been required to do this before, and they feared it would take up time they didn't have. So they circumspectly went up another level to my superior, Roland. He listened to their concerns and neither contradicted nor sustained the weekly report requirement. His passive action left them feeling he had authorized them to not support the reports, because he didn't sustain the effort. Over the next few weeks, things digressed as the team members found reason after reason why the report wasn't working. They didn't like the formatting, and in general resisted the effort, to the point where I finally suspended the effort. Yet even though it was dropped, it left a seed of frustration in the entire team which took more time to resolve.

This would have worked much better if instead Roland had sustained the request by asking those who came to them the simple question and statement, "Did he ask you to do it?"

Perhaps a reluctant answer, "yes."

Followed by his simple sustaining statement, "Then do it."

If Roland had any concerns, he could have brought them directly to me. With this corrective feedback and understanding, I could have then couched the request to the team in a more understandable manner. I could have solicited feedback from the team to learn how they might be able to help me alleviate my fears, but in a manner more acceptable to them. However, without this sustaining cycle, the overall effort faltered and fell apart.

It can be more overt than this, however. I was once in a meeting where Erin, a project manager, was leading a conversation with customers. Isaac, an engineer on the team, raised a question and asked, "Perhaps we could review the original designed use cases, and it might -" at this point then Erin cut him off and declared, with some emotion, "I don't see any value in that, at all."

The room was quiet, and things were a bit uncomfortable. The message was clear—Erin was closed to input, her mind was fixed, and she had no respect for Isaac. This disrespect changed the rest of the tone of the meeting, and not for the better.

Sustainment goes all directions. If somebody is discussing or presenting information that feels contradictory to your understanding or belief, the wrong course of action is to correct them in front of everybody, and it is even more wrong to circle around to their audience afterwards and solicit their thoughts (see: *Dangerous Allies*). Regardless of your position in the organization, this corrodes relationships.

As a leader, in addition to sustaining your subordinate's choices, it is important to recognize the chain of command downwards. It may seem useful to side-step one of your direct reports and work with their own subordinates, but when you do this without their involvement, you undermine their influence.

In any scenario where there is a difference of opinion, the best course of action in the moment is to leave the original assertion without contradiction. It is rare for somebody to say something so damaging it cannot be repaired at a later time. Follow up with a private meeting to reconcile the differences. Work through things with the individual, using empathy, to learn the reasons behind their position, with an ear to the fact that yours may be the wrong belief.

Importantly, if a correction must be made, the same individual who made the incorrect assertion should make the correction. This is the person who reaches out to the original audience and clarifies their mistake.

This last step is extremely important. If a somebody made a mistaken claim, gave an improper direction, or perhaps just was working in a direction you disagreed with, then stepping out and making the correction yourself will geld them.

Empowering them to correct the situation, on their own, strengthens your relationship with them and strengthens their relationship with their peers.

As a leader the process of sustainment downwards is crucial. Sometimes, a common tactic to avoid direct confrontation is to encourage peers to act in conflict. This is demonstrated with a scenario where an executive, Mara, wished to enact a change to how her organization worked, but did not know how to make it happen because most of her direct reports liked the process already in place.

Furthermore, the responsibility for this process was delegated to Beverly. But Mara had found an ally. James, a peer to Beverly, sympathized with Mara's desire to change the process. She then encouraged James to act contrary to

Beverly's authority, yet did not communicate this direction to Beverly. James felt empowered because Mara had given him direction on something they both agreed upon. But his actions usurped the authority of Beverly, creating confusion and friction in the organization. Beverly then acted to elevate visibility to the friction with meetings and discussion that further frustrated everybody over an issue they felt was already resolved. Beverly was confused, asking Mara why James was being so 'political.' The overall result was fear and stress on the entire organization.

The problem here was not Beverly's or James' in how they dealt with the situation. It was Mara's lack of respecting and sustaining Beverly, and she also missed most of the principles discussed in the section *Delegate with Success*, while also falling into the mistake of seeking *Dangerous Allies.*

The simple process of Sustainment creates a chain of respect that works all directions. If you want respect, you must give respect, both up and down the chain of command, as well as with your peers.

Consider through your working career if you have seen any of these scenarios play out. Have you perhaps ever acted in a manner that may have lacked sustainment to your direct reports, your peers, or your superior? Were there other ways that you could have accomplished your goal, and sustained them instead?

DELEGATE WITH SUCCESS

Handing off work in a clear manner that strengthens a relationship is challenging. Yet delegation is something we all want and need to do. We recognize that we cannot do everything, but it is hard to pass off important things to others. Can we trust they will do it right? Or they will do it at all?

Delegation comes with a deeper conflict: we need to transfer ownership of a problem to somebody, yet at the same time, we know that if they fail to execute well enough, the ownership comes back to us. It is this paradox that can lead to us subverting our own success.

To avoid this problem, try to remember three things when delegating:

1. **Instruct** – Clearly explain what you need, without saying how it should be done.
   - Define the result or product, without worrying so much about the details.
   - It is good to suggest ways it could be done, to help the person understand the scope, but do not proscribe the 'how.'
   - Make sure the person understands that the delegation has happened.
   - Make sure the person knows how they are to report on their progress, and completion.

2. **Respect** the person and let them do it their own way!
   - They will do it differently than you would.
   - If you are genuine in delegating, then you must let the person act with freedom to do it differently than you.
   - If you focus on the deliverable, then the method becomes less important, giving them the ability to own the task themselves.
   - For many, this is the most important, yet hardest part.

3. **Report** – Check-in with the person and allow them to report on their status, regularly, and when they are finished.
   - Listen with the intent to understand, not to respond. Sometimes miscommunication of a report may be on the listener (you), not the reporter.
   - Make sure to recognize the person's best effort, even if it is not everything you expected. Somebody who feels appreciated will be motivated to improve. This is not the same thing as rewarding any result, regardless of success or not (which is something to avoid).
   - If they do not know how to report on completion, then you have not completed step #1 properly.

With an understanding of these three key points, think back to your own successes and failures in delegation, either on the receiving or giving end of the Relationship. It is likely you can identify numerous cases where simply adding one of these steps to the process would have greatly improved not only the delegation but the overall Relationship.

Communication

Communication is the key to keeping sound relationships. Communication is the lifeblood that pulses through the relationship. Without it, the relationship will fail.

Imagine, if you will, a long stretch of desert highway that seems to go on endlessly in both directions. Now place in the middle of this road a group of your favorite IT co-workers, mixing both technical and management. Which direction would they go, if they had no further instruction? Would they wander off into the sagebrush? Or would they pick one direction over the other?

You can be assured that some sort of debate would likely arise over who knew the area, some gadgets would be consulted, and there would be a lot of fear and uncertainty. But perhaps they could agree on a direction, and the group would somehow manage to all move together.

However, what happens when this group reaches a fork in the road? Do some of the technical people believe they should go right, where others believe they should go left? The group pushing to go right may present many good reasons, but these reasons are very technical in nature—things about prevailing winds, standards of highway construction, and best practices. However, the group wishing to go left have the same types of arguments, and both seem to hold merit.

The manager who was able to get everybody heading the same direction the first time is now at her wits' end. She no longer knows what to do. Both groups have very good arguments—at least to her ear.

Members of both groups have become crusaders. Each has decided they are right and are fighting for their cause. Meanwhile, the manager is left in the middle of the mix, not wanting to take a side. She likes all of her technical people and is afraid to choose sides.

The situation only gets worse if there are two managers, one for each group. Now the manager doesn't need to choose sides, she can just go where her team wants to go, and if the other team goes their own way, then it is their choice, not hers.

This is the world of poor communication, with no planning or architecture. There is no goal on the horizon, and for all that the managers can tell, their technical people speak Klingon. The manager doesn't understand Klingon, and with the rapid rate of technology change, they don't have the time to learn it.

The value an architect can bring to the communication arena is that of a trusted translator. Architects are individuals who can speak both technical and management. The architect can be a neutral party who can translate the Klingon of the technical individuals to the managers, using needs and deliverables instead of tools and standards, so the managers themselves can come together and agree on the plan (the right or left fork).

Furthermore, the architect can help the managers come together and find the fence post on the horizon. They can all, together, decide which direction is desired at large, have it documented, and then, when the fork comes up again, the discussion is much easier to handle.

In the end, if a customer does not understand or agree with a plan, it is not the customer's fault; it is the architect's. Architects facilitate the creation of the plan, which makes them responsible for the communication. They are responsible for understanding the needs of the customer and all other actors in the scenario (program managers, project managers, and the like). If communication of change is failing, architects should work to improve it in a manner that helps the customer to feel validated and recognized. When the plan must change, it is in accordance with everybody's needs.

Three principles help with communication and being a trusted translator: **Know Your Audience, Be Concise,** and **Know Your Material.**

KNOW YOUR AUDIENCE

Before you present any information, take time to know your audience. Understand their fears and interests. Then tailor the conversation to where their interests lie.

I once sat in on a vendor roadmap presentation to a busy Director. The conversation started well. Everybody was lively and engaged. But then the vendor began the same presentation they had repeated uncountable times before, with deep technology explanations on every slide. The Director's eyes glazed over, and an hour later, after it was over, he had no questions. The presenter did not tailor any of the information to what the Director cared about, and the result was an hour of wasted time because in the end, the Director took nothing of value away from the presentation. All because the vendor didn't take time to understand his needs. This Director was not interested in technical deep dives; he just wanted to know the high level explanations and answers to the questions of his own fears (how would the vendor's product help him close projects faster).

Spend time to understand your audience's Primitive Needs, and tailor your conversation to match what the audience cares about.

BE CONCISE

Knowing something is much different than simply believing something. I can believe it will be sunny tomorrow, but know it was sunny yesterday because I was there. The difference is based in an undeniable certainty because it is something I have experienced.

There is something in all of us which drives us to love what we have come to know about technology. The things we know are based in endless hours of investigation, contemplation, blood, sweat, and tears, and we have the battle scars to show for it. After these trials and tribulations, we feel emotionally invested in what we know. With this knowledge, however, comes a passion that can lead to lengthy technical conversations that perhaps our audience does not care about.

Although this is as much a part of knowing your audience as anything else, we need to remember to focus our statements on the message we are trying to convey. As much as we may find it elegant to use a base32 encoding over a base16 encoding, our audience may not care about the particulars, other than it saves on space which will result in bandwidth savings. Instead of explaining the nuances of base32 and base16 encoding, just state that you have discovered a way to cut the size of the data.

Remember, we love what we know, and we cherish this information, but others may not share our perspective. As much fun as it is to talk about these things, what does our audience need to hear?

KNOW YOUR MATERIAL

I once had a CEO tell me after I struggled to explain a problem facing our organization to his satisfaction, that if I cannot explain it to him, then I must not understand it myself. This statement rocked me a bit. I felt I knew the technology—and it was unfair for him to draw such harsh judgment. I left the meeting wrestling with the challenge. Perhaps it was him who just couldn't understand the technology? I thought of explaining Calculus to a sixth grade student just starting Geometry—I would have no greater success in teaching that student Calculus.

Eventually I realized he was not challenging my technical capability. He was challenging my ability to know his needs, fears, and to be concise. I couldn't explain the challenge we were facing to him because although I understood it at a technical level, I didn't know what it meant to the organization's plan, needs, fears, and deliverables.

I came to him with no options for changes to any direction. I was just presenting a problem with no options, and I wasn't being concise about it. I was explaining the technical limitations as well as I knew them, but I didn't know how these limitations affected our customer's needs, let alone our own.

Knowing your material is not just understanding something at the technical level—it is getting into the deeper nuances of the way all the needs are being met by the technology. Knowing how to install a system is only the first step and is often the easiest. Knowing how it will be effectively integrated and used by your customers—that is the challenge.

Analysis

Analysis looks at the big picture, breaks it into digestible chunks, and considers solutions. The ability to understand a complex system in its entirety is critical to an effort, but can be difficult for many people. Effective analysis involves decomposing the complex system into smaller components, subsystems, and parts. This decomposition enables all others aspects of Design, Architecture, and Strategic Planning, because to build a proper plan, we must first understand what we are trying to do. This cycle of analysis through decomposition of a deliverable into its constituent elements is something we all do every day of our life, even if we are not good at it. It is critical to making a plan, and how well we do it determines the success or failure of any endeavor.

Consider a simple situation—a weekend outing to a campground. We know the need (to go camping), but we may not know what else to do. We have to consider things backwards—we start with the goal and think about what it takes to get to that point. First, we need camping gear (tents, cooking utensils, etc.) We need a method of transportation that can handle all of the gear and people, a destination, a list of activities we may do while there, and all the other incidental needs such as fuel for a vehicle and our cooking source.

If we don't properly analyze the situation, we may miss something. Some things, if forgotten, may not be a big deal—if we don't have a plan for what to do while at the campground, we can probably just wing it. But what if we forget to bring matches? One critical item, if missed, can become a major problem later.

Two key elements can help in properly analyzing a situation: Understanding **Primitive Needs and Constraints**, and proper **Decomposition** of the work effort. Using a **Work Breakdown Structure** enables both.

PRIMITIVE NEEDS AND CONSTRAINTS

A *primitive* need or constraint is simply a general need or constraint described at its most basic level. Finding the primitive needs or constraints is an important step to analyzing anything from a simple problem to a complex challenge. If we miss the primitive need or constraint, we will waste time and effort.

As an example, we had a team working on a project that listed information in a database. After making a routine change, the customer reported that they could no longer see their data. We convened an emergency council to discuss the problem. It appeared that, before the change, the user would filter their query with a shortened three-character string. This showed them exactly what they wanted to see.

The recent code push included some significant performance increases by reducing unnecessary data transferred between the server and the client, and the data for the three characters was removed, in the name of efficiency. As the dialog transpired, suggestions were offered, yet all centered around fixing the immediate problem (the inability to filter with the three characters) rather than finding a solution. The suggestions varied from reverting the entire change, to re-coding the change, and including just the piece of data the client wanted.

What we missed, however, was the Primitive Need. It wasn't until we dug into the Primitive Need as a question when we realized there was a bug involved. The customer didn't have a need that involved typing three characters to see their data—that was the requirement being discussed, but not the Primitive Need. The Primitive Need was to have a method that allowed them to see only their data (framed as a question, it would be, "How do I see only my data?") We eventually looked back on the original design and realized the original deliverable was to use a different filter. But apparently that filter was not working, and somewhere along the line they had discovered that the three characters gave them what they wanted.

Once we recognized the primitive need, we asked ourselves: why wasn't the original filter working? That is when we discovered the bug: the data was broken before it went into the database, so the way the customer should have searched would not work. The fix was three lines of code in an entirely different system.

Had we not spent time to consider things at the Primitive Need level—to think about it as a solution, not a problem fix—we would have fixed a problem that didn't need to be fixed, while wasting work effort, and creating more complex code. Furthermore, we would not have discovered the actual bug until much later.

Although the difference between a Need and a Primitive Need can seem subtle and slight (such as needing to type three characters to filter, vs needing a method to see their data), it is about the way we approach things. Are we fixing a problem, or finding a solution? This difference is critical in providing effective and efficient results to our customers.

Tools that can help identify the Primitive Needs and Constraints are: **the Multi-step Why** and **the Critical Question**.

The Multi-step Why

When writing a story, there is a tool authors can use to find a compelling motivation for a character: *the Multi-step Why*. Essentially, after coming up with an initial character motivation, the author immediately asks "why?" and tries to find a deeper answer. The reason this is useful lies in the fact that the first thing we think of is usually too simple, not hitting the real point, or cliche.

For example, remember the story of the boy Cole at the creek picking a flower. If we ask no questions, we have only a shallow understanding of what is going on with him, and we don't understand the relationship involved. So we ask ourselves, why is he picking a flower? The first answer is: his sister likes the flower. While that is interesting, it is still not the primitive reason. So we ask again, knowing his sister likes the flower, why is he picking it? Because she is terminally ill.

Getting better. And we ask again: she is sick and likes flowers, but *why* did he feel compelled to pick the flower then and there? Because he hoped that the flower she likes—that he carefully picked from that special creekside that he knew meant so much to her—would bring her happiness amidst her suffering.

This exercise helps us to better understand the Primitive Need of the boy. It is rooted in his fear of losing his beloved sister, and his need is to find some way to help her. Prior to asking the questions of why, all we had was a boy who wanted to pick a flower.

Be careful, however, when using the multi-step why. If not properly phrased, the questions can come across as an attack, which is the opposite of the intent which is to better understand the person's needs and fears.

A team member, Jean, came to me once and stated that he just couldn't see any way the tool I had asked him to investigate could do the job we needed. Without thinking too much about it, and while walking briskly to a meeting, I tersely asked, "why?" I earnestly wanted to understand why he felt this was the case. I wasn't trying to question his judgment. The truth was I wanted to learn what insights had brought him to that decision, but I was also in a hurry and not giving him the time and focus he deserved. He reacted with a defensive, "well, because it just isn't able to do what we need." So I asked again, "why?" Jean's body language immediately shifted to the defensive—he folded his arms and stepped back. Fortunately, I was able to recognize my mistake and explain what I wanted—to understand how he came to that conclusion. Once that was out of the way, he was perfectly happy to open up and explain his thoughts.

The Critical Question

The purpose of the Critical Question is to help us focus on a need by phrasing it as the question being answered, rather than as a statement of want. This simple exercise helps to direct our thoughts toward the fears being addressed, which brings us closer to the Primitive Needs, rather than the problems.

To demonstrate the difference, we had a customer, Jade, who was happy with an old tool and resisted changing to a new tool. She made statements that the new tool would not work for her, and every time anybody asked her why, she brought up arguments explaining her general requirements—to have a series of reports made by her tool—without getting to the primitive concerns—the content of the reports. The conversation always stalled with Jade's assertion that the new tools could not provide the reports she wanted. She was a crusader talking about the technical merits of her tool and the time she had invested, and she didn't want to address the effort involved in changing. Therefore, it became an emotional response.

I met with Jade and discussed what critical questions she was trying to answer, without talking about the technology. We found there were several for each report—not just one. Once we had the critical questions phrased in her words, it enabled the conversation to move forward, and we could engage him in discovering if the new tool could answer her needs, or not.

Identifying the Critical Questions helped Jade to feel recognized and to feel that her needs were validated. We were able to set aside the technical statements encumbered with emotional baggage and focus on alleviating her fears of not being able to deliver information to her customers.

DECOMPOSITION

The process of decomposition involves understanding the desired outcome, then building backwards from that outcome to the current state. It is the process of taking a complex work effort and breaking it into smaller and smaller manageable chunks, until the total scope of what must be completed is understood. Decomposition and needs go hand-in-hand.

The best way to address decomposition is to think of the end result or desired outcome, itemize individual deliverables that compose the overall end product, and then iteratively analyze each of these, again reducing where possible into their constituent elements.

Using deliverables as the units for decomposition helps to focus the mind. Behind each deliverable can be any number of tasks—but tasks are a distraction to the decomposition process. Deliverables can be scoped at many levels. They may be parts of a whole or the final result.

Deliverables are not needs, requirements, tasks, or features. Deliverables fulfill a need, and aspects of a deliverable are features. Multiple features in combination come together to make a deliverable. Furthermore, in the project management context, deliverables are not 'User Stories' which are a specific construct of Agile process control, written by the customer to describe their 'want' (which is not necessarily the same thing as a need). User Stories also include the customer's role, the benefit they see and acceptance criteria as part of the definition. If anything, deliverables are the resulting product that ultimately resolves the User Story.

Because nothing is easy, the matrix of Primitive Needs can have both internal and external deliverables, each with dependencies upon the other. Do not underestimate the challenge of internal deliverables. It is such a challenge that the light-hearted term *yak shaving* has formed in the technology industry to categorize these internal deliverables. This term covers all the stuff that needs to be done to resolve the problem, but may not seem directly related, from an outside perspective, and may be considered wasted effort because it is not immediately evident how it relates to the final deliverable.

For instance, to build a website, one must first build the servers and ecosystem that will run the website, along with a system and process for maintaining the website. These all must be designed and implemented before the website goes live, and during the process additional things may come up, such as how the servers are monitored, backed up, and secured. But the customer doesn't care about the earlier steps—thus, they are internal deliverables, and spending weeks getting these internal deliverables completed is considered a process of yak shaving. Furthermore, it is often easy to spend more time yak shaving than is required, and that is why it is important to scope your internal deliverables as well as your external ones. Technical debt often comes from internal deliverables, that were missed in the planning cycle, and skipped for fear of yak shaving.

This understanding of the needs, how they map to deliverables, and how the different deliverables live in a matrix of dependencies is used in the process of decomposition. The result of the decomposition can then be used to scope the work effort. To do this, there must be a rough concept of how to implement each deliverable and the work effort behind it.

Finally, over time, the process of decomposition is repeated, adding definition. Consider the vehicle analogy, where the steering mechanism was given as a deliverable. At the start of the effort, the scope of the deliverable is defined loosely—a need for a mechanism to steer the vehicle. During the implementation cycle, there is an internal process in which the needs for the deliverable are considered, and a solution is designed, engineered, then implemented. Depending upon where you are in the effort—the timeline of the project—the deliverable improves in definition. At first, it was general—a need for a steering mechanism—but as it is designed and engineered, it becomes more clear. Tie rods, couplings, and mechanisms are figured out, ending with the final deliverable and a very understandable blueprint. This is an iterative process that refines and improves upon the documentation around a deliverable until it is complete.

The end result of a properly decomposed analysis should be a clear understanding of the entire set of deliverables required to finish the work—but not necessarily the specific details of how to do the work (the distinction is explained in *Phase 3 – Execution: Understanding Project Management*).

Proper decomposition to the level of detail required for your effort, and no further, is a critical component for the success, because it provides the reference DNA of the project. Everything is measured against this basis during the execution and controlling project phases. Much like double-entry bookkeeping helps to keep ledgers in balance, a properly defined decomposition of deliverables can provide the balance to ongoing tasks and scheduling efforts, and it also helps to avoid building technical debt. Without clearly understanding what you are going to do, how do you know if you accomplished it?

A few tools or principles may be used to help in the decomposition effort: **Cross-Cutting Concerns, Loose Coupling,** and **Abstraction and Normalization**.

Cross-Cutting Concerns

Those things interdependent between systems are cross-cutting concerns. These are technical demands or attributes that affect multiple needs. They are the broad qualities of a system that have a systemic impact across many needs or constraints. Simply put, cross-cutting concerns are those things which cannot be simplified any further, and which impact more than one system.

A few examples of common cross-cutting concerns may help:

* **Security** – how all parts of a system are secured, using authentication, keys, or other mechanisms.
* **Monitoring** – the need to know if any component of a system is working properly, as well as if the entire solution is working properly.
* **Logging** – centralizing all data, so it can be usefully mined, by planning how all systems store their logs.
* **Patch Automation** – the way updates, patches and changes are handled using programmed automation, rather than manual work.

Locating cross-cutting concerns helps in the analysis and decomposition of a system, because the process of finding cross-cutting concerns also helps identify the Primitive Needs. Yet, frequently, these cross-cutting concerns are glossed over early in an effort, with cry's of 'premature optimization' or 'analysis paralysis.' Unfortunately, this just leads to a last-minute discovery and frenzied implementation of missed concerns right before go-live. This often results in poorly made compromises, additional technical debt, and a much more complex and difficult-to-sustain system, as the cross-cutting concerns are ignored, while each discrete system does its own thing.

Loose Coupling

Loose Coupling is the idea that a component of a system has little to no direct knowledge about the attributes of another component. Loose coupling is essential to successful abstraction and simplification, although some would argue it can create more complexity. This is the paradox of loose coupling, in that it is an abstraction which can both add complexity, yet also simplify. It enables modularity through abstraction, and it facilitates finding *Cross-Cutting Concerns*.

Loose coupling provides flexibility and enables easier division of work effort, because parts of the effort can be isolated to a less complex system. It is easier to meet goals by working on a smaller scale, within a defined set of parameters.

This flexibility also means if one component of a system must be replaced or updated, the change does not impact the entire system—just the one part. For example, in the new micro-service software movement, complex systems are decomposed into small, loosely coupled applications, each providing a small service. It is easy to update and maintain these small, discrete systems individually rather than coordinating a large update.

Considered another way: is it easier to plan a haircut for four hundred rambunctious toddlers at the same time, or just one?

However, many vendors intentionally create tightly coupled systems, because loose coupling is not in their benefit. If you can easily swap a vendor's product with another, the vendor must provide greater value as a standalone component.

For example, in the world of programming, if you are building two systems that exchange data, describing that data abstractly through a simple API allows for loose coupling. However, off the shelf tools, such as ORM frameworks (object relational mapping), can relate the data directly against a database. While this can speed the effort of implementation dramatically, the result is a tightly coupled system, where the data shared exactly matches the columns of the database on one side of the relationship.

With this scenario, any changes to the table structure directly impact the data interface shared between the hosts. If you want to add a new column or change the name of a column on the table, you must also change the connecting system. Because of the tight coupling, you now have to coordinate and change two or more systems, instead of just one.

With loose coupling, on the other hand, you to define an abstract structure for data that is shared between components. You don't stress about matching the data to the table layouts. This creates loose coupling and also facilitates more optimized back-end database features.

Though loose coupling may seem like a challenge specific to the programming world, it is a valuable tool in all aspects of decomposition and design. Vendors may resist loose coupling of their tools and will always assert that their tools work best when coupled to their own tools.

In my experience, after implementing many products both ways, I have found those vendors who promote loose coupling and address a cross-vendor market strive for a higher level of excellence, because they must, in order to stay competitive.

Abstraction and Normalization

Abstraction and Normalization is known by many names, some good, some bad. It is a tool that is part of our everyday life—we use it whenever something is too complex for us to understand. A simple form of it is stereotyping, where we use abstraction to find common attributes across a large population of data.

By looking at things in a simplified manner, we can take something complex (such as a population of millions) and select a few attributes which matter (such as hair color and weight). This allows us to reduce the large population of millions to a manageable set of twenty or thirty.

This very reduction of dependencies is why we so often reach into the abstraction toolbox when trying to understand and analyze systems. When looking at a complex set of needs, it is easy to become overwhelmed by cross-cutting concerns that seem to get out of control.

For example, if you have a data set of two million people, each with sixty attributes, then looking at each attribute individually to find commonality is daunting. But if you dig into the Primitive Needs and discover that all you really care about is hair color and weight, you can then abstract the data set by summarizing hair color and weight, and you can stop worrying about all sixty attributes.

With this exercise of abstraction, high level attributes group needs together, allowing one to consider them as a single item, instead of trying to address the entire solution all at once.

An example of abstraction helping us to understand a situation came up when we faced the challenge of reducing approximately 20 vendor products in an organization. On the surface, they all seemed to compete in the same space, but they also all had differentiating value. Each product was brought into the organization based on the specific needs of a group within the organization, and reconciling everybody's needs seemed nigh impossible.

After reviewing all of the products, we discovered they all focused on three Primitive Needs, and after abstracting and reconsidering cross-cutting concerns, we realized the data we really cared about could be distilled into two attributes. At this point, we had something all of the applications could be measured against—how well they meet Primitive Needs and two data elements. Coming to this point was not easy. It involved many conversations to help understand the value we were getting out of each application. Or, effectively, what fears were being alleviated by using the application.

However, abstraction can also be bad, if not done when properly considering the reason for doing it. Sometimes people abstract simply to remove duplication, and this can lead to greater problems if people are not aware of the overall needs being addressed. The key of abstraction is to recognize the cross-cutting concerns, identify the needs being met, and focus on loose coupling.

WORK BREAKDOWN STRUCTURE

A functional tool to help decomposition analysis is the Work Breakdown Structure (WBS). Originally defined by the US Air Force, it has since been refined by various Project Management disciplines. For a simple explanation, it is a hierarchical listing of the deliverables, where each element is described as a product, not a task, and each sub-deliverable must encompass 100% of the work involved in making its parent.

For example, in building a bike, the wheel assembly would include the wheel, tires, and brakes, but not the steering mechanism. Although they are related, they are different work efforts, connected at a higher level. The distinction of what becomes a different deliverable is made by how much rough work effort is involved. Continue to iterate and break down each deliverable into simpler and simpler elements until each encompasses 80 hours or so of work.

This relation of work effort to deliverables can introduce confusion, however, and it is easy to slip into thinking about tasks and schedules. A good Work Breakdown Structure is about scoping deliverables and outcomes, rather than defining the steps to make it happen. To maintain this distinction, it is best to label each element as a product, outcome or deliverable, and not as an action or processes.

For example, to define a server deployment effort, one might use:

1. Build Prod and Dev Servers
   1.1. Create Server Automation
   1.2. Build and deploy Servers

However, that is an action oriented list of tasks. It is better structured without adjectives as:

1. Servers for Prod and Dev

The assumption is now that all of the work required to deliver servers for Prod and Dev is encompassed under that deliverable. If needed to be decomposed further, it can be broken into sub-deliverables as:

1. Servers for Prod and Dev
   1.1. Functional Server Automation (tested)
   1.2. Development Servers
   1.3. Production Servers

But while doing this, you realize that with 'Build and deploy Servers' in the first list you were thinking of server automation, not application delivery. You have identified potential technical debt! You revise the list:

1. Servers for Prod and Dev
   1.1. Functional Server Automation (tested)
   1.2. Functional Continuous Application Delivery (tested)

1.3. Development Servers

1.4. Production Servers

Although the change may seem slight, it keeps the intent of the WBS focused on deliverables, instead of tasks, and this helps it to fulfill its role throughout the project as a balancing tool, regardless of the project discipline being used. Furthermore, reorienting the mind to think in this manner also helps bring other needs to light. We already identified the missing application delivery component, but if you notice, in the second example we decided to change how we listed server automation—it was not sufficient to just have it made, but we realized it probably should be tested and functional if it had to stand on its own as a discrete deliverable. Breaking out Development and Production was also useful, because they can be delivered at separate times.

Understanding the differences among a need, a deliverable, a feature, and other project management elements such as user stories and epics is critical in making a WBS valuable. Adding the WBS to the project management process can also be the difference between the project effort remaining on track or failing. It is more critical in Agile projects than Waterfall, as a WBS can help maintain the general direction without having to fully complete all plans. To use a WBS with Agile, iteratively add detail to your deliverables as they approach the current sprint.

Team Baselining

Teams come in a variety of flavors, each with their own challenges. I have worked with teams that click and hum like a well-tuned machine, and others that misfire and stutter. Teams most often fail to work well together because of fear. Team members don't understand their role, or they feel their own needs or their customer's needs are not being met.

A Team Baseline meeting is an effective exercise when this stuttering is happening, or when there is an org change, to help alleviate fear. Everybody is brought into a room, and an open-dialog 'roundtable' atmosphere must be established. If the atmosphere of safety cannot be properly established, and if people hold back their input—either by fearing each other or where the result will end up—then the meeting will not be productive.

Listen for crusader dialog—if it is being used, then that team member is likely in a defensive posture, which is not productive. If individuals are more interested in explaining problems, but not in making concessions themselves or owning a solution, then the right atmosphere has not been established.

There are three phases to a productive baseline meeting: **Discuss Fears**, **Discuss Needs**, and **Discuss Roles**.

DISCUSS FEARS

This can be a dangerous meeting for some people, as they don't like to admit to being weak or uncertain. The best way to frame this is to ask each person to consider what it is that concerns them in their ability to get their job done—perhaps even before coming to the meeting. Set the stage that they can safely express these fears and concerns, even if those fears or concerns might fall outside of their job duties. Nobody will censor or critique.

A leadership individual should set the atmosphere by starting the process. It works by using a whiteboard (no computers) and listing each individual across the board, with their concerns or fears underneath. For example, John, a project manager, may list that he is concerned about meeting deadlines, that people might not be as productive as they could be to help meet those deadlines, and that he is afraid of getting off track with the schedule. Morgan, a developer, worries about building the right solution for a customer, having enough time to do the work, and being able to keep the current system running while also making new changes.

During this phase of the meeting, do not discuss needs, methods, fixes or solutions. Only discuss worries, concerns, fears, or those base things that drive each individual. Leave a space on the board between each individual for a second column. The board may look something like the first example on the following page.

Baseline exercise board example #1:

John
_____

meeting deadlines

people's productivity

getting off track

Morgan

right solution

having enough time

sustaining current

Discuss Needs

After the conversation around each contributor's fears is complete, move onto discussing needs. Fears drive needs, so this is a fairly simple exercise of rephrasing fears as needs, in a question form. John defines his fears simply as, "Is everybody working effectively?" and so forth.

As the fears are being converted into needs, overlap can be identified, and some consideration can start around what roles each person should hold. This might then look like the second example.

Baseline exercise board example #2:

John	needs to know
meeting deadlines	is everybody working effectively?
people's productivity	what to work on?
getting off track	can we make our schedule?
Morgan	needs to know
right solution	what do our customers want?
having enough time	what to work on?
sustaining current	is there enough time to also keep current systems running?

Discuss Roles

The tone of this conversation should be constructive, with the entire team engaging to determine how everybody can help each other resolve their needs and fears. This is the final stage where people discuss if a need is appropriate for an individual, or not, grouped into Roles. Sometimes many individuals can share needs, and other times it can be decided that an individual no longer should worry about something because that is already being covered by somebody else.

Discussing roles can be a frightening step for some leaders, because people approach role definition with different purposes. Commonly, these fall into one of three categories:

- The **Limited Use** perspective, or, "this is the square I sweep," along with the assertion that nothing outside of that square will be swept, even if it is one inch away.
- The **Authoritarian** perspective of, "I need to know what I do, so I can act unilaterally in my space and not have to worry about other's needs." But that is never a good place to be—there are always relationships and interdependent needs that are at play.
- The **Shared Lifting** perspective, or "knowing what everybody is doing helps me know where I can fit the best or help the most."

The Shared Lifting type is the most beneficial, but is easily mistaken for the Limited Use or Authoritarian perspective, when people start to ask for Role Clarity in an unsafe environment. The root of the Shared Lifting perspective is empathizing and understanding each teammate's needs and fears, so the team at large can all contribute to the work effort in the best way for the individual's capabilities. That isn't to say the individual should not go beyond the defined role, but it gives people a place of comfort to work from. It also helps to ease their own fears, allowing them to be a more productive contributing member to the team and reducing overall clunk in the team dynamics.

A final note: Shared Lifting is not necessarily equal lifting—some people will be able to contribute differently than others. Knowing where our strengths and weaknesses lie helps everybody to work together better. The team should strive to be able to have a conversation unhampered by pride, and that in itself is a challenge.

Handling Resistance

Resistance is a natural reaction to poorly planned change, and it is driven by fear. You will see the most resistance during the Empathy phase of Design Thinking, as people start to recognize that change is coming, and they are inclined to act from a place of fear. We all resist change when our fears are not recognized and the plan is not understood.

The first impulse each of us has, when faced with resistance, is to push back. It is common to meet force with even greater force.

During this time, be extra vigilant and remember the basis of fear that we work from. A few tools to help: understand **Ownership and Negativity**, and be aware of **Dangerous Allies**.

OWNERSHIP AND NEGATIVITY

While ownership and negativity may not seem like related topics, they are one in the same. When somebody takes ownership over something, they stop considering it in a negative light. Yet people who are unwilling to own a situation are willing to pick it apart. They provide any number of reasons why something will not work, without owning the actual solution by suggesting ways to fix the problem and offering to do the work themselves.

❝ *When somebody takes ownership over something, they stop considering it in a negative light.*

The lack of ownership may be a subtle and difficult thing to detect, because in general we are very good at disguising our actions in the trappings of proper behavior. In one effort, Ranbir, a developer, worked on a user story, backed by a use case. He provided the deliverable and handed it off to the customer. The initial sign off seemed to work well, but during testing the customer noticed part of the required solution was missing, and asked Ranbir about it. His response was to defer. He felt the customer's request was a new feature, and asked the customer to submit a new request. Ranbir's own pride crippled his ability to help the customer; and he could not admit he had made a mistake. The customer was frustrated because he felt it was not a new feature, and the work should have been part of the initial request. It was scoped in the original use case, and Ranbir did not own the situation. He punted it with the trappings of process—go submit a new feature enhancement request. How could he be a negative contributor, when he was following the process? Yet the customer was left hanging.

A proper method to follow using ownership would have been for Ranbir to empathize with the customer. He could have investigated their claim, assumed they were right, and tried to find out what he may have done wrong, regardless of how much work he had put into things up to that point. If what they really want is outside of the use case, offered to help them with completing the submission of the new feature request.

This lack of ownership was based in fear. Ranbir did not want to be negative, yet his actions came out as negative despite his efforts. He was worried about meeting his own goals, and he was afraid of looking like he made a mistake. He was afraid that if he had to stop his new work and go back to the original task, he would fall behind. His fears became a barrier to his ability to have a positive relationship, and instead damaged the relationship.

DANGEROUS ALLIES

Sometimes we just want to find a friend and 'vent' because things are frustrating. This can be dangerous, however, and can create toxic relationships, because of how it objectifies the other person. Consider the interaction:

Joe steps into Sue's office and rolls his eyes, "Pat's insistence that we need to use his tool is really creating a problem. I sure wish he would wake up and realize the world has moved on."

Sue nods in understanding, "I know, I just heard from Don who thinks the same thing. What should we do?"

In this example, consider the context that Sue and Joe are peers of Pat. So, why are they having this conversation without Pat? No amount of discussion at this point will solve the frustration that Pat is causing, because he is not there, and the two talking without him cannot determine a solution. Yet this is a very common pattern, and it is what we do when seeking Dangerous Allies. Joe is trying to find people who agree with him before taking on the fortress of resistance that is Pat, rather than trying to empathize with Pat and understand his fears.

Sometimes one does need to let off some steam, and sometimes it is seeking Dangerous Allies. Be careful in the type of dialog you are having – it may be that you are the individual introducing toxic behavior into the workplace.

A better response for Sue may have simply been, "Have you asked him why?"

Empathy – Define

During the Empathy Phase you spend time Defining why you are working on the challenge. This is when you outline your objectives at a high level, to provide the framework for the remaining steps. You need to understand what you are challenged with, to be able to find a solution. To complete this step, remember the following:

- Identify the issue to be solved, described as close as possible to a *Primitive Need*.
- Identify all *Customers*.
- Agree on a priority, framed in terms of urgency and when it is needed.
- Know what success looks like. What is your completed state?
- Take time to discuss your glossary of terms, to avoid *Conversational Dissonance*.

Empathy – Research

While *Defining* your challenge, you should consider all aspects of the challenge through *Research*. Investigate many things to avoid functional fixedness, where you feel only one solution will work. This includes:

- Decompose the needs, at a high level, to understand the scope.
- Review history—previous attempts in-house and external attempts or studies.
- Identify past obstacles. Why did they cause problems before, and what was the outcome? What was learned?
- Find your critical people relationships. Who are the thought leaders in your organization? Who are your supporters, investors, and critics?
- Find your technological relationships, to reduce technical debt.
- Discuss the challenge with your Customers.
- Identify existing competing solutions already in place in your organization and their value, including history and what can or cannot change.

PHASE 2 – CREATIVITY

" In the beginner's mind there are many possibilities,
but in the expert's there are few

— Shunryu Suzuki

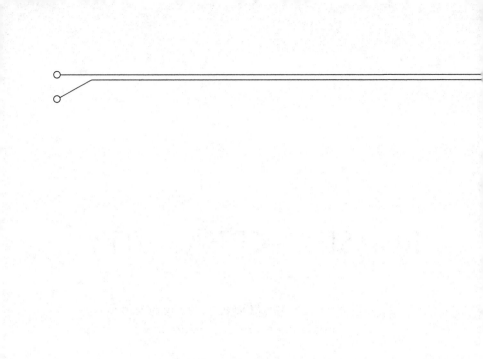

The second phase of *Design Thinking* is *Creativity*, when your thinking shifts from Empathizing with the problem, to considering ways it may be solved. Creativity flows best with little resistance. To help this, the time spent in *Empathy* is important, both *Defining* and *Researching* the challenge. There are two steps to this phase: **Ideation** and **Prototyping**, which can be worked iteratively.

Ideation, at a high level, is a shared session of creativity, similar to Brainstorming, but improved. *Prototyping* is the exercise of exploring an idea only as much as is needed to determine if it is viable. To be most effective, strive to think out of the box and seek powerful ideas – tools to help with each of these steps are described throughout the rest of this section, and at the end we will summarize the key elements of each step.

Meetings

Meetings are critical to good communication and maintaining relationships, and are a required part of the Creativity phase. However, they can also be a negative force in your work effort, not only hurting productivity and velocity, but demotivating people.

There are volumes written on the topic of having productive meetings, and I suggest an exercise to research them and use what works best for you. With design, it is important that meetings and communication happen in a productive manner, so I will spend a moment to cover this topic.

We should recognize that good meetings are amazingly helpful, but bad meetings are more than just bad. They can be destructive. However, suppressing meetings in general, to avoid bad meetings, is also wrong because it hurts relationships. We, as creatures, need to communicate, and that is what meetings are about: building relationships.

Meetings considered to be bad are usually so because bad meetings waste time on an individual's behalf, which puts them into the wrong mindset, and this feeds negativity. Not only have they wasted time they could have been spending being productive, they spend time thinking about themselves, their lack of work progress, and even discussing the wasted effort with others and fostering a negative mindset which spreads through the organization.

The challenge we face is that too much structure around meetings can also become a burden. However, is it possible to find a good balance?

Consider asking everybody who makes a meeting to do three things:

1. Choose one Format for the meeting.
2. Set Topics for the meeting and let people know ahead of time what to expect.
3. Limit Invitations.

Of these three things, the Format of the meeting is often disregarded, yet is very important. This establishes the type of conversation you expect ahead of time so you can conduct matters quickly and efficiently. There are a few common formats to meetings:

- **Ideation** – The Ideation type meetings are those where the conversation is to help figure out 'what' it is you want to do, but not necessarily getting stuck in the 'how.' However, these meetings typically discuss things at a very high level, and are different from Planning meetings. During Ideation, you are discussing possibilities for deliverables, where in Planning and Tasking you already know what is being delivered. As Design Thinking is showing us, these are critical meetings to have earlier than later in a process, yet are often skipped, causing frustration as things have to be changed later in the process.

- **Planning** - Planning Meetings contain the strategic discussions around deliverables that are already designed (if only roughly – the output of Ideation), but are not yet into the Tasking phase. Typically, in a Planning meeting, the stakeholders discuss high level implementation plans.
- **Tasking** – Tasking meetings are tactical, focused around who is doing what work, how the work is progressing, and the other elements of task management. Depending upon the makeup and size of the team, it may be common to combine Planning and Tasking into a single meeting.
- **Understanding** – This meeting is for building relationships. You focus on thinking outsideof yourself, and understanding each other's needs and challenges. This is a highly valuable meeting to help synchronize between teams or individuals, but it is important to only focus on understanding, not solving. Scrum stand ups are a form of Understanding meetings, but they can also be something like sales presentations as you consider a vendors' offerings.

Takeaways from this meeting can create other meetings to help solve the problem. An easy approach to an understanding meeting is for everybody to discuss only those things which are at risk to their success or other's success. Feel free to list accomplishments or things that are going okay, but do not spend time on them. You may also simply ask, "how are things going?"

- **Team** – Team type meetings build or discuss things not covered by the above.

Marketing and Statistics

Many statistics can be twisted to sound good or bad—depending upon the desired outcome of the analyst. Unfortunately, in the world of limited time and rapid change, a situation is created where you need to spend more time learning the technology yourself, rather than relying upon a vendor's claims to performance—which are often clouded through misinformation and the desire to make a sale. You need to understand your architecture, as well as the performance or capacity requirements you have.

If you are in a meeting where new technology is presented, and at the end of it you are more confused than at the beginning, you need to remind yourself that clarity is the enemy of deception, and statistics are the greatest tool of both. If you want to get to clarity, you must understand how to use statistics properly.

Benjamin Disraeli, a 17th century literary figure, stated that, "There are three kinds of lies: lies, damned lies, and statistics." This same sentiment was further elevated by Mark Twain and is used to explain how easy it is to be persuaded by numbers and statistics, as well as the tendency of people to ignore or disparage statistics that do not support their preferred point of view or position. In the IT industry, statistics and marketing information are deftly wielded on a daily basis, and developing the skill to see through the smoky room they create takes some effort, and experience.

It is important to understand your technology and not to just trust in the vendor's opinion or tools. For example, consider a scenario from 2008. We supported a sizable enterprise, and we were considering the latest multi-core technology from two different major CPU manufacturers, specifically investigating how each performed in various load environments. One of these manufacturers had numerous published reports about their stellar performance (after years of falling behind), and they were receiving great press about how well their platform was performing over their competitor's. Their numbers seemed quite compelling and were made with reputable testing software.

---

66 *It is important to understand your technology and not to just trust in the vendor's opinion*

Our tests, however, showed the opposite. We discovered that, when run in a real world scenario (simulating heavy database load) the vendor claiming improved performance instead was 50% slower than their competitor. Not only this, but the competitor's CPU had half the cores.

These results were scandalous. Who were we to question the Marketing Results—directly to the manufacturer? We made certain our results were carefully documented and then had several months of meetings with everybody, including the virtualization vendor, the server manufacturer, and the CPU manufacturer's engineering team. Each party wanted to blame the other. Our configurations were first blamed, then when the configurations were found to be solid, the server hardware was blamed, or the software, and so forth. After months of working through this issue, we ended up on a conference call with the CPU manufacturer during which they admitted two things:

1. The tests they ran and published were with their special compiler, using their special libraries. We ran our tests with a real-world compiler, using off the shelf libraries and options—exactly as anybody else in the field would run things.
2. Their system "might" have a bottleneck with the specific type of load scenario we had (heavy I/O), where the published tests avoided I/O and instead focused on light I/O tests. And, of course, their new CPU had fixed this problem.

These results were very enlightening and helped us to make educated purchasing decisions.

Marketing challenges like this can be easily side-stepped by considering two key rules of statistical science: margin of error, and sampling procedure. If a statistic is properly calculated, it should include a margin of error. In its absence, there is only speculation backed by no scientific method; or in other words: opinion. Second: any time you see a statistic, look for a definition of the population sampling procedure used—statistics used to sway a person's thinking do so by hand crafting the population sample, thus getting results to the desired target. Consider this promotional statement from 2011:

> [Microsoft is] #1 in databases, putting huge pressure on Oracle (just announced a layoff of 10,000) [Gazelles Insight 14-July-2011]

This is a classic type of PR release bandied around in the religious crusades of IT. It is uplifting for the Microsoft camp and seemingly demoralizing for the Oracle camp. However, it does not speak about the population sampled to determine what #1 even means. Is it a random sampling of every database in the world? Likely not. Is it a random sampling of Microsoft customers? Does it include only commercial databases? Or does it provide a weight for the size and transaction load of the database? Are the vast forest of small office franchises running Microsoft SQL server given equal weight to the largest websites in the world which do not?

The Illusory Truth effect is the psychological tendency that exists in each of us to believe information to be correct, merely because we hear it more frequently, whether it is true or not. Marketing propaganda feeds into this by providing highly subjective statements that mislead us into believing what is stated is actually true.

Understanding that this effect exists is helpful in putting vendor claims at arm's length.

These examples just reaffirm there are lies, damn lies, and statistics. There is always an angle when somebody is trying to convince you of something, and their motivation usually does not align with yours. Be careful when somebody tells you statistics of any type, and take the statistics with a grain of salt. Feel free to trust what somebody tells you, but do yourself a favor and verify it yourself.

Status Quo is not a Reason

Where status quo exists, there is likely somebody harboring fears around change. One must accept that with technology, change is a key factor, if not a constant truth. Being able to embrace and adapt to change is what makes a person compelling and vital to an organization. Those who dig in and resist change become roadblocks, impediments, and ultimately less valuable. They defend their territory with nothing more than "we have always done it this way." But status quo should never be a reason for resisting change. This is a challenge to be carefully balanced, because in Design Thinking we want to consider past experiences and empathize with the problem. But those experiences can easily become excuses to do nothing, protecting the status quo.

The Golden Tool

There is never a single 'right' tool for a need. However, there are many wrong tools. For a variety of reasons, technologists tend to slip into the mindset that the tool, process, framework, or methodology they have found is the 'right way' of doing things. By exclusion, all other tools are then 'wrong.' The earlier conversation about technology crusaders describes the symptoms of this problem in detail.

> 66 *There is never a single 'right' tool for a need.*

The prevalence of such a mentality is a constant force to struggle against, where technology choices are presented as the right way, or the wrong way. Remind yourself that there are many ways to build something, each of which is acceptable and valuable. Just because one way has been done up to now, or you did it a certain way in the past, or that you believe one way is correct—this doesn't mean that there is no other way that would work.

Proper needs analysis and focusing on function, not tools, helps to avoid these problems. But there is more to it. A poorly designed tool, even if it meets every need defined, can be a wrong fit because it is difficult to integrate with, runs on a different platform than your team supports, or is poorly designed and difficult to use.

When tools are considered as a commodity and you are faced with many options, your focus becomes removing the ones that are problematic for your organization's constraints. The conversation then shifts to a powerful stance where you can consider the business needs in the most effective way possible.

We tend to look at it backwards, however. The statement 'best of breed' is often bandied about, as either a negative or positive thing depending upon what the speaker is pushing for. Best of breed can proliferate the Golden Tool concept that there is only one 'right' solution. However, its inverse is also a fallacy—some strategic plans intentionally work to avoid best of breed arguments, and this can also lead to the wrong tools being selected.

The best way to frame the conversation is by asking the questions:

- How does the tool's strategy align with our strategy?
- Can the Vendor be a Partner?

The second question is as important as the first, because, even if the Vendor doesn't currently align with your strategy, by being a Partner and not a Vendor (discussed later in *Rationality*), the Vendor's tools can work with you, towards your strategy. Find the best fit for your organization, and avoid the Golden Tool.

COTS, In-House, and OSS

When considering tools there are often three available options: vendor supplied (aka commercial off the shelf / COTS), in-house (building the solution yourself), and open source software (OSS). Each of these comes with its own baggage, and everybody has their preference. Here are a few experiences to promote clarity and success when these conversations arise.

The category of COTS can be expanded to include SaaS or other vendor hosted services, as well as tools which are vendor-supplied but you install yourself. For the sake of comparison, I am grouping each of these into the same label. The general challenge with COTS is finding the best tool to exactly meet your needs. The value of having a vendor-supplied solution is that the vendor is responsible for problems, fixes, and upgrades to the tool itself. Much of this book's content is specifically about how to match tools to needs.

The world of customization creates a challenge. When building something in-house or using OSS software in a COTS manner, you can adjust the software to meet your needs exactly. With an in-house solution, you just build what you need. With OSS, you can extend and expand an existing solution to meet your needs, because the source of the tool is available.

However, this can be a tar-pit, if you are not ready for the effort that comes along with owning a customized tool. The lure of 'no licensing' is a tempting proposition, but it might be a fallacy when the Total Cost of Ownership is considered. The first step is to factor a TCO around all options, when considering building something in-house, including development and sustainment labor (see *Total Cost to Own*).

The second step, if the choice is made to go down a customized route, is to compartmentalize. A common mistake occurs when the team resolving the need is also the team implementing or customizing the solution. The same individuals are both the implementers and the customers. The melding of roles can lead to a breakdown in ownership and visibility of the application to the organization at large.

For example, engineers and technicians frequently bring OSS software into an organization on the side, to meet their needs. These implementations quickly become strategic to the organization, yet also fail the organization, because of how they were introduced and how they are sustained. This typically happens when engineers and technicians are unable to communicate and relate their needs to management, and so they just 'make it work' by finding an OSS solution and integrating it into their work. Management usually finds out about these incidents so far down the road that the product is too valuable to remove, yet it is also consuming great amounts of labor to support.

There are two problems in this scenario. The first is the disconnect between engineers and management, typically symptomatic of Design Thinking missing from planning. The second is the combination of the implementer also being the customer, which creates a conflict of interest. The individuals end up struggling to prioritize their work—fix or update their tool, or work on helping their customer?

When an application is introduced outside of the organization's normal processes in this manner, it takes a backseat to the other applications, simply because it is outside of the norm, and thus it is not visible. The organization has processes and methods around owning and managing tools, yet the customized tool has circumvented all of these.

Ideally, in the right situation, a customized tool can be valuable when COTS tools struggle to meet the needs. Properly understanding the Total Cost of Ownership and compartmentalizing the development and implementation of the tool is critical in the success and integration into a strategy for the that tool. This compartmentalization and separation changes it so the customer (the team using it) has the same relationship to the solution as they would with any other vendor, and now ownership of that tool aligns to processes within the organization.

Simply put, any custom solution should be treated in the same manner as any other vendor's tool. The customer interfaces with a different team, which owns the development and support of the tool, even if the customer is your own organization.

Creativity – Ideation

Ideation is not Brainstorming, although the approach is similar. The general concept of brainstorming is functional, in that many minds together can think of stronger ideas than when individual—yet the defined method for brainstorming tends to create banal and plain ideas.

With brainstorming, the assertion, is made that there is never a bad idea, and nothing should be criticized—do not judge nor debate. The belief is that when people are criticized, they tend to shut down.

However, the belief that all ideas are good ideas is wrong. There are ideas that just don't work, and in a brainstorming session where you cannot think critically, many of the ideas stop at the first thing which comes to mind, and these are often cliché ideas.

Adding the *Multi-Step Why* helps to clarify what could be cliché and get to the root idea the person may not have even realized they were proposing. The idea may be grounded in a solid primitive idea of value, but what is discussed is not yet there, and if left unquestioned in the moment, it will never get there.

The key is how communication is worked during *Ideation*. People should come in and check their pride at the door, and they should approach the conversations with empathy to understand each other. If people are waiting to respond, and not listening to understand, it is the wrong conversation. Every idea should be considered, but that doesn't mean every idea is a good idea.

129

During Ideation, people should be able to debate merits and dissent, as long as it is done with humility, empathy, and honesty, not pridefully pushing agendas or position. The point of the dissent and questioning should be focused around understanding the person's idea, not tearing it down.

Rules and tools for Ideation:

- Bring a notepad for each person.
- One topic at a time – this is the most challenging, and is the reason you brought a notepad. While people talk, you will have your own thoughts. Write them down, circle around to them as time allows.
- Use only empathetic dialog:
  - Listen with the intent to understand, not reply.
  - Positive not Negative: negative statements shut down the creative flow and are resistive.
  - Descriptive not Prescriptive: statements like "I liked this part of your idea" or "I don't understand this part" instead of "This part of your idea might be better if it was blue" or "If you made this thing green, I'd like it better." Let the idea creator choose and alter elements of their idea, and you just ask for clarification.
  - Be willing to accept people asking the Multi-Step Why of your own ideas, with a recognition that they are just trying to better understand them, not shoot them down.
  - Don't be a crusader

- When considering ideas, if somebody is resistive but cannot explain why, try to discuss what their concerns might be, and seek to understand what lies beneath the resistance.
- Avoid functional fixedness – think out of the box, consider other angles to the problem.
- Review ideas from outside sources (collected during Research phase).
- Generate as many ideas as possible.
- Select the most powerful ideas to Prototype.
- Record everything and review your notes.

Creativity – Prototype

Prototyping is the rough exploration of an idea, piloted or developed only as much as necessary to determine viability. This is when functional models around success are analyzed, such as a Total Cost to Own, including labor and all other parts of the picture.

Principles of prototyping:

- **Throw it away** – Whatever is prototyped should never become production. To enable rapid exploration, prototyping should discard common processes that provide stability and value but can encumber speed. The idea of throwing away work can be frightening to some, but it empowers the prototype process. The challenge faced is often people see a functional prototype, and then wish to call it production.

131

- **Avoid artificial limitations** – Try things that may be prohibited. Just because you cannot do it now doesn't mean you shouldn't explore. For example, if your organization has a rule against using Cloud technologies, that doesn't mean you shouldn't evaluate them during prototyping. If the value proposition exists, perhaps the rule can be reconsidered.
- **Do not fear failure** – Thomas Edison once said, "I have not failed. I've just found 10,000 ways that won't work." Constantly evaluate your progress and be willing to pull the plug yourself if you are not getting closer to your goals. Identify sooner than later if what you are doing is not going to work.
- **Define the Minimum Viable product** (MVP) for each prototype, and only build to that level. This should be the smallest increment you can identify to better understand the need.
- **Create and present working prototypes**. Have short iterations with working examples and demonstrations at the end. Each engineer or developer should be able to show the results of their effort. Even if it did not end in success, there is something to learn.
- **Seek Feedback** from a diverse group of people, including your end users and detractors.
- **Clarity is the enemy of *self*-deception** – seek truth, not emotional judgment that may be deceiving yourself. Don't let pride cloud your judgement of

your success. Use facts, not emotional dialog. An example can be pulled from a comparison of technologies where each team submitted their pros and cons. One team member stated that the tool he preferred was beneficial because, "Team X has always maintained control of this service, and we want to make this choice because it helps us to wrestle control away from them." This was not the most productive statement.

- **Clarity is the enemy of deception** – make sure your reports and calculations are clear and concise, to portray the truthful story. Avoid power adjectives (wrestle, grievous, struggle, monstrous). Just as with emotional dialog, these can be triggers for others receiving the report.
- **Document and report your findings**.

PHASE 3 – RATIONALITY

    Architecture is not an inspirational business, it's a rational procedure to do sensible and hopefully beautiful things

– Harry Seidler

*E*mpathy and *Creativity* are both very exciting, but at some point delivery and reality must enter into the picture. This is the Rationality phase. This phase includes three steps: **Choose, Implement,** and **Learn.** To help with these steps a few tools are identified, and at the end we will summarize.

Baselines, not Standards

In the IT industry, the word "standard" is loved and cherished. It is within easy reach in our toolbox, it fits snugly in our hand, and we use it on a daily basis, wielding it like a sword in both offense and defense. Our standards are the body and composition of everything we have researched, discovered, and decided is good. But it is a dangerous word, because it does not mean what we hope it means.

We discuss standards all the time, like they are the holy grail of solutions—if only 'they' would conform to our standard! Standards have a time and place, perhaps in an industry that doesn't change quite so frequently.

66 *Standards become a form of chest thumping and assertion of authority.*

Imagine if the metric measurement standard changed the definition of how long a meter is every year. It wouldn't be much of a standard. Yet we persist in using this word in the technology industry, with hopes that it will carry the same weight as it does in the general world.

On some level, based on our usage, the word standard could probably be replaced with "My Way." Standards become a form of chest thumping and assertion of authority. The statement, "Sorry, your app/service does not meet the standard," perhaps may be better stated as, "Sorry, your app/service is not built the way I like to see it built."

The biggest problem with the word "standard" in IT is that it comes with an authoritarian disposition of inflexibility, and this inflexibility damages relationships. The word is a very easy scapegoat when a customer comes to us with a difficult need. Consider a real world scenario: if a builder of houses said, "We have standardized on brown shingles. So... sorry, every house we build must have brown shingles. We have built all of the other houses to this standard, and we need to keep them the same."

The sword of standard wielded in this statement feels extremely arbitrary to the outside. There may be very valid reasons for having it—perhaps there is a great discount on the brown shingles, and using something else would cost more. Or perhaps the color itself somehow has extra qualities in the environment of these houses. However, to somebody wanting to make a choice it just feels artificially limited and argumentative.

We put up roadblocks, talk about standards, and make the customer's life difficult, when in reality they are just trying to get their needs communicated. We have failed them at this point, because they cannot comprehend why we are arguing over shingles. They don't care about shingles, standards, or anything else we bring up. They just want a new house and don't understand what the big deal is with brown shingles.

Whatever the case, with this simple statement of standards, we feel it is no longer our fault—it is just the standard. We try to cast ourselves as the victim right alongside the customer. But do you think the customer believes us, let alone cares?

There are places where standards are appropriate, although in most cases, a better word we could use to avoid the conflict and help us to empathize with the customer's needs is 'Baseline.' When this simple change is made to the organization's vernacular, it has an immediate change to the approach people take in understanding and empathizing with each other.

A Standard is inflexible and focuses inwardly on our needs, not those of the customer. Either you are meeting the Standard, or you are failing to meet the Standard, and there is no room for conversation. A Baseline, however, is something you compare against.

How close are you to the Baseline? Do you need to diverge? Let's discuss the total cost impact of that divergence and see how we can make it work. Suddenly, we are in a world where our processes is focused on our customers and helps them, instead of hindering them.

This is how we change the conversation from a hand wringing authoritarian, "may I please do this thing?" relationship to a more beneficial authoritative, "I have this thing, could you help me figure out how it could work?"

When Implementing, take care to use Baselines, not Standards.

Total Cost to Own

Calculating the Total Cost to Own (TCO) over a three to five year period is a form of Business Cost Analysis useful to bring clarity to a situation confused with statistics and crusaders. TCO should factor in all aspects of labor, software, maintenance, and any other incidental costs. The three to five year term helps because it is a factor of the entire lifecycle of the product.

I once had a vendor who tried to circumvent and RFP review process by offering his company's software at no charge. They were a major contender for the space, and all we had to do was agree to sign up for maintenance over the next three years. He was so eager that he even sidestepped standard channels and made the offer directly to our CIO.

We restrained his earnest approach and continued with the product comparisons in the review process by calculating TCO, including labor to support and sustain, as well as hardware requirements. On the surface his deal appeared the best—who can argue with free software and just the cost of maintenance? To make things worse, the most technically viable candidate was extremely expensive up-front . . . yet there were appearances of labor savings. Figuring out the TCO was difficult. We had to build a model that covered the rate of activity or change while using the tool and how much labor would be involved in each change. Then we had to get a committee of stakeholders from across the organization to all agree with the estimates, and we further reviewed the model with each vendor, taking into account their own thoughts and perceptions and adjusting to suite.

During this process, one of the vendors initially balked at our calculations for the labor effort with their product, thinking we were too high. Our model resulted in 120 hours per work or change effort. So we asked them what it should be and walked through each step of the model, reviewing each of the factors we had identified. After taking their suggestions for each of the factors, the sum total estimate came in at 180 hours, instead of our original estimate of 120!

After the dust settled, the final TCO comparison painted a fairly clear picture. The vendor with "free software" ended up at a $20 million TCO over three years, where the vendor we finally selected, which seemed the most expensive up front, was only at $9 million TCO.

TCO brought clarity to a situation that began in a very confused manner.

Execution

> 66 *Vision without Execution is Hallucination.*

-Thomas Edison

Thomas Edison's statement summarizes how useless planning can be if we do not have the ability to bring the results to fruition. Making forecast statements and suggestions about industry direction is an academic exercise that will bring you no closer to delivery, if there is no understanding of how to work between where things are now and the desired future goal.

Analysis helps you to understand the broad scope of possibilities, but not necessarily how they work within the constraints of your own business needs. A plan helps you to define and communicate the direction you want to go, but during Execution you determine the effort.

Consider an eighteenth century battlefield—if the general were to stretch his troops around all sides and declare a simultaneous attack on everything all at once, he likely would fail. Just having the troops does not mean success on the battlefield. Instead, the general begins by considering the most appropriate place to apply force.

Design can be a drive-by process where a plan is put into place and the Architect leaves. However, when an Architect is not part of the iterative cycle of execution, when something is unclear or changes must be made, it is easy to lose sight of the fence posts on the horizon and change direction, even in minor steps.

I worked on a development effort that had expanded its developer team. Some of the newer developers were not aware that, early in the project, the database relationships had been roughed out at a high level. Although the definitions were incomplete, there were several tables roughly defined yet unused, with the expectation that they would be refined later in the work effort. At one point, a new developer started to have a need for some of the additional tables, but he didn't understand how they were to be used. He just wanted to fix his immediate need and add columns to the table he was working on, instead of referencing the alternate table, because he was unaware that this broke the relational models in place.

For the non-technical explanation, we had a series of buckets for data, each with a lid that only allowed certain sized blocks into the bucket. The blocks he had worked on up to this point were all square, but now he had to work on round blocks. Rather than looking around to find that there was a bucket for round blocks, he wanted to retool the lid on the bucket he had used so it would allow round blocks as well as square blocks. This would have resulted in a dirty database, where data was stored inefficiently (or a bucket with both round and square blocks, when we wanted them sorted by shape).

Fortunately, with the cycle of design as part of the project, we noticed the change of direction early on, and were able to educate the developer as to the use of the alternate tables, saving on re-work in the future.

While it is possible to design the entire blueprint from top to bottom up front, it is not necessary, and frankly it is a monumental challenge in the constantly changing world of IT. This is why the Waterfall/Designed process control model, to use project management terminology, can be so difficult in an IT setting. However, the flexible Agile/Empirical process control models can easily disregard design. If running a project where the end definition is refined over time, to enable early delivery and facilitate flexibility of changes, then Design Thinking should also be a part of that ongoing cycle if you wish to hold any hope for a resulting product that meets the customer's needs and actually finishes with success.

Because needs change, Design Thinking provides value when used in an iterative process through the life of an effort to understand how changing one part of a project will affect the other deliverables. A plan that considers needs of the business whole and is reconciled iteratively along the way helps to meet deliverables and execute effectively.

Without proper execution, we spend excessive effort changing technology, without improving the posture of how we are helping our customers. Design Thinking is most effective when it is invested in the execution process.

Partners not Vendors

I have had the pleasure of working with a variety of amazing partners and vendors—but what is the difference between the two? I never gave it much thought until a friend asked why we identify the two differently, and it comes down to the relationship. A vendor is a one-way relationship. They are interested in selling you something. A vendor cares if the product works for you, but generally only up to the point that you purchase the product. They are not invested in making sure you get continual value out of what they are selling—and, honestly, this is a by-product of the rate of change and failure in the IT industry. Although a vendor knows their product can do what they purport it will do, the vendor cannot guarantee you will be able to make it work in your organization, with the wild variety of influences and challenges that may exist.

A Partner, however, is genuinely interested in your success with their products. But it is difficult for any vendor to invest in your effort at a meaningful level, as everything has a cost.

Finding vendors that can be partners is a steep challenge, but when they are discovered, they can be relied upon as part of your strategic direction. You rely on them being a pivotal part of your strategic plan. Rather than just identifying a need, you identify a product, but only with these partners, because you have a level of trust that their offering will be something that will adjust with your needs going forward. You can trust that even if their product in the current day is not where it should be to meet all of your business needs, they have your interests in mind, and they are working towards fulfilling the same needs you hold.

There are a few indicators which can be used to identify a Partner versus a Vendor: **Feedback and Features, Internal or External Innovation, Principles of Design, Balance of R&D and Sales, No Lock-In,** and **Maturity.**

FEEDBACK AND FEATURES

Does the vendor have an easy channel to accept feedback and feature enhancement requests on their product, along with a track record of executing on these for anybody beyond their top five customers? This sort of company usually has a customer council where they invite customers yearly, if not quarterly, to a forum to discuss how they are using their products and solicit feedback on future direction.

Does the vendor easily expose their internal program managers and architects? Transparency to the engineering cycle indicates a Partner, not a Vendor.

INTERNAL OR EXTERNAL INNOVATION?

Does the company have a history of slash-and-burn acquisitions, where, rather than innovating their product internally, they buy new products and cobble them together with bailing wire and duct tape? Or, if they do acquire, do they rewrite and retool the acquired product to fit within their existing framework? Products that are retooled are much easier to sustain and support, and this can be an indicator of a Partner, not a Vendor. Those companies interested in seeking improvements to their products by acquisition and bolt-on are less interested in meeting customers' needs and more interested in checking the box on their product portfolio.

PRINCIPLES OF DESIGN

How evident is a strategic plan in the company's direction? The strategic plan can be an indicator to where the company's investment and interests lie. Can they provide a Roadmap beyond a quarter or two? Do they have a 3-year plan they are building towards? These do not have to be tactical in detail with specific features and dates. They very well may be high level strategic goals. However, having some of these indicates vision, architecture, and the principles of Design Thinking at play.

Some companies may have a Roadmap that is highly detailed, but the details are immaterial in value. Minor fixes and tweaks described over the next year are just as bad as having no plan at all.

Together these can be used to discover the company's investment and interest. Are they milking the product line and padding their quarterly reports until the next acquisition, or are they actively innovating and providing new value for their customers?

BALANCE OF R&D AND SALES

Where does the company place its value—in Research and Development, or in Sales and Marketing? Some vendors are notorious for acquiring a product, firing the development staff, and leaving the product to wither and die while they collect support and maintenance—at least until the next acquisition is found. These are not products that make for a good strategic match, and those Vendors with this reputation usually make for poor Partners.

NO LOCK-IN

Does the product require vendor lock-in? Products that require additional vendor solutions to 'work best' are benefiting the vendor more than the customer. These are lock-in products and provide the vendor supplementary leverage to make it more compelling to use the rest of their portfolio. In the end, they become much more difficult to extract yourself from later. On the surface, it may appear to provide value. Perhaps there is a quick ramp-up, or the reports are all glowing. But after the TCO is run, it only provides the vendor value (bladecenters and tightly integrated hardware to network stacks are often in this category).

Partners are willing and open to work with others vendors, and they are leaders in providing open interfaces and following open standards (instead of embracing and extending a standard). Does the vendor send somebody to a standards board because it would look bad to not be on it, or did they push for the creation of the open standard and fund its development, as well as contributing some of their own technologies to seed its survival?

If you have ever had the conversation, "We already have vendor X, so just adding one more of their products will be easier," then perhaps some consideration as to the overall value of the lock-in may be in order.

MATURITY

How is the company on a maturity scale? New startup companies can be exciting, but may be acquired and shelved, or they may fail to gain traction fade away. Vendors who are past the 'green behind the ears' phase are still fresh and invigorated, and usually meet most of the Partner requirements, without the danger of imminent acquisition. Those vendors who have become monolithic through building a massive portfolio are also often the hardest to work with as a Partner, as they cannot navigate their own internal bureaucracy, let alone help a customer to navigate it. This isn't to say it is the rule, but conventionally, the larger a company becomes, the less flexible and understanding of a customer's needs they are.

Process vs Delivery

The amount of tooling, automation, and process built into a deliverable must be decided up front and defined as its own deliverable. Trying to retrofit a process or system to change how it is delivered, automated, and tested is in itself a project.

With so much change and fear around implementing solutions, it is easy to forget the processes and plans around sustainment and delivery. However, mid-implementation is a poor time to make changes to whatever processes were planned.

The amount of effort we spend working out operational readiness, processes, testing, and automation is equal to or greater than the amount of time we may spend on the actual implementation itself. The risk of changing things mid-implementation must be understood and can critically impact the success of the project within the original projected timeframe.

To demonstrate: Melanie came into an existing project as a developer who held a high level of trust in automated testing and deployment. At the time, Continuous Integration was just coming into the limelight. Many tools were available, as well as many references to success in using these tools and processes from notables such as Google and Facebook.

However, the project was defined as a short-term effort, to be built once by a team of one to three developers, and then left to run with minimal sustaining effort required. To add confusion to the mix, the defined scope of deliverables did not include process and testing definitions—these were assumed to be very lightweight, because of the lack of need for ongoing perpetual changes and the small scope. This was compounded by a lack of project documentation around change control.

Therefore, when Melanie recommended adding Test Driven Development (TDD), her arguments seemed sound—this is how Google did it, after all. She felt the changes wouldn't take too long to implement, and they were approved. But her definition of TDD included some additional processes: Extreme Programming (XP), which included Continuous Integration (CI) and multiple lanes of development. These new ideas were created in the industry for large sites with massive programming teams all working on the same code base, supporting a product that changes daily—not a small internal website that would be delivered and largely left unchanged.

This created much contention among developers as she ripped the shared environment apart in trying to implement her vision of how things should work, using her perceived authority for the approved change (TDD) to unilaterally coerce into place heavyweight processes (XP and CI), and completely paralyzing the ability for the team to deliver to the customer. After the dust settled, the project delivery was set back five months and another developer quit the team, refusing to work with Melanie again. The team's morale was in shambles.

In the grand scheme of things, this five months may be okay, or it may be unacceptable. But recognizing and understanding the total breadth of what is involved before the change to process is implemented is the crucial component. It may be better to stay with an existing process, as inefficient and inelegant as it may be, rather than to disturb the existing plan, until the change to the process itself can be integrated as one of the future deliverables.

A definition of the project scope of all deliverables, both internal and external, should include processes and automation. Changes to these should follow the defined project change control, so as to properly communicate to all invested parties the ramifications of the change to their expected delivery plan.

Continuous Change

Like Sisyphus, damned to push an enormous boulder up a hill each day only to watch it roll back down, those of us in the IT are compelled with a similar burden in the way we classically manage software. We relate to the exhaustion that Sisyphus must feel while looking down the hill—which, in our case, is a major version upgrade to our software. This should be a moment of triumph, which lasts about as long as it takes for the vendor to release a new update, and the boulder is back at the bottom of the hill.

The situation worsens, because not only do we have to maintain the software we care about—pushing that boulder up the hill for eternity—but our backs are also burdened with the increasing weight of regulations, compliance checks, audits, and eldritch security requirements.

Is your system current in all governmental regulations? The acronyms just keep coming. Each one brings an albatross of research into new technology you didn't plan for, nor do you have the staff to properly investigate.

Do your information protection measures meet all of the latest security standards? Are you properly auditing and reviewing your operational procedures? Each of these added burdens requires you do more with less. Your staff cannot keep up.

Maintaining software in the modern world is an exhausting saga equal to any of the horrors of Greek mythology. But it doesn't have to be.

There are two related tools to use in addressing this: **Continuous Delivery**, and **Never Upgrade**.

CONTINUOUS DELIVERY

Continuous Delivery is the act of breaking break big changes into many small updates done frequently, while using an automated system for making the change, which can test and verify there were no problems. The boulder of Sisyphus with Continuous Delivery becomes a stream of small pebbles. If one of them is dropped, it does not roll to the bottom of the hill, and it is easy to pick up and recover.

Changes which would typically require a major version update are carefully stitched into the update process, so they can co-exist with existing features—sometimes even supporting a 'feature flag' where the update is live, but not seen, until you want to turn on the new feature. In this world, you also *Never Upgrade*.

NEVER UPGRADE

Do not upgrade software.

This statement may seem so entirely contrary to any modern notion of computing that it feels ridiculous, but it is a principle I learned through implementing many large-scale sites and ERP systems. An upgrade is not a patch. Security, bug, and other patches are still relevant and should be applied regularly, but at some point, the service needs major foundational upgrades, usually every few years.

Do not do it.

To shift from one major version to another is usually a fairly involved task that can cause much risk to the customer. It is the boulder of Sisyphus. As such, the simple assertion is to avoid any major version upgrade.

So, how do you keep current?

If you cannot use Continuous Delivery to make the change safely, and a major update is required, then build in parallel. This is the *Scorched Earth* approach.

When a new major version comes out, create an entirely new environment for the new version. Migrate the data and configurations only, then run in parallel for a period of time, after which you can cut-over when all issues are identified and resolved, and then spin down the old environment (burn it down – ergo *Scorched Earth* is left behind). This also has the added benefit of having an immediate and simple fall-back, in the scenario that the cut-over goes wrong.

Rationality – Choose

Choosing is using clear data points to make a decision for implementation. Avoid consensus thinking during this phase of consideration, set aside emotion and ownership or pride over ideas, and divest all emotional baggage. It is important to find the right solution, not just the one with the most passion behind its proponents. Principles of Choosing include:

- Set aside emotion and ownership of ideas.
- Review each option in the context of:
- Meeting the primitive needs.
- Aligning to the overall strategic plan.
- Risks to success (external and internal).
- Measuring against the defined success criteria defined in the *Empathy* phase.
- Remember the most practical solution is not always the best solution.
- Propose a clear and simple plan with options, to the decision makers (consider TCO).
- The plan should be concise and tailored to the audience.

Rationality – Implement

Implementation is where the actual work is done to bring the solution to reality. In IT this is where we often start, without understanding what needs we should be solving. Yet ignoring design principles may be the root cause as to why so many projects fail. It is hard to do design properly, as it requires we face the fears that bind us; but when we do proper design, we have greater success.

There is no perfect process to Implementation. The key is to pick a process that fits your team and effort, make certain everybody on the team understands and is invested the process, and stick with it, unless it is clearly not the right process for your team. Do not try to implement without having a process to document the tasks and objectives, as well as a process to monitor and manage your progress. Implementation is about accountability, which can only be had when you know how you are going to Implement.

Many people bring up the challenge that the time taken in design can be arduous, and the luxury is not available—it is easier to just 'do something,' waving the Agile manifesto. However, I would rather spend more time in design and have more projects succeed in Implementation, than to skip design and have most projects fail to deliver, or languish and meander, slowly being overcome with technical debt like an aging ship encrusted with barnacles. When done properly, the time invested in design will make for a quick and painless

Implementation. In my experience it is this simple: those projects which apply design principles succeed, where those that do not apply design principles fail to live up to their expectations.

Rationality – Learn

One of the biggest trials I have witnessed with Agile project methodologies is that they run as a persistent effort that has no end, and they can easily slip into just the *Implement* phase, without considering *Empathy* and *Creativity*. While this seems to fit much of the world we work in, it only perpetuates the mistake we so often make, which is to forget to look back and learn from our experiences, let alone setting a future deliverable.

When done right in an Agile world, the results from Learning should feed directly into the next iteration's *Empathy* phase. But without Learning from our successes and failures, we are apt to repeat them.

Learning should include **Measure**, **Review** and **Report**, discussed fully on the next page.

- **Measure**:
  - Evaluate if the outcome met its objectives.
  - Gather feedback from all actors: customers, implementers and vendors.
  - Review relationships from all actors.
- **Review** documentation for completeness:
  - Standard Operating Procedures (SOPs or Runbooks).
  - Structural, Behavioral and Execution Architectural Documents.
- **Report**:
  - Discuss what could be improved. What worked? What did not?
  - Document and find ways to bring these into your future iterations.

PREPARING FOR CHANGE

> 66 ...the reformer has enemies in all those who profit by
> the old order, and only lukewarm defenders in all
> those who would profit by the new order
>
> – Niccolo Machiavelli

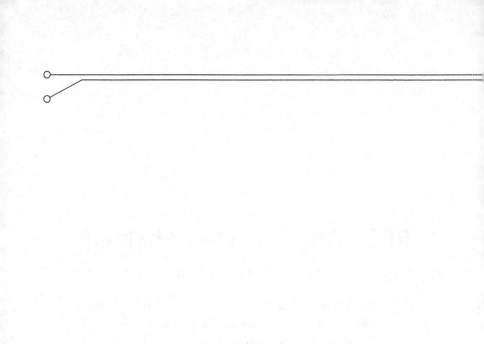

Design Thinking is about making effective change, but before change can happen, one must have a solid foundation of support and understanding within your organization, in process, stakeholders, and all of the people who will participate.

The Silver Bullet Process

Can a problem be fixed simply by adding more process? Not usually . . . so why do we tend to do it? Adding process is a common response when we are faced with a challenge we cannot handle or wrap our heads around. There are processes to help you be more agile, structured, lean, transparent, or accountable—whatever the adjective, there is likely a process for it.

However, without understanding the reason something is not currently working (likely based in team member's fears and perhaps your needing to better empathize with them), throwing a process at it will only aggravate the problem, not fix it. Processes such as project management disciplines, testing methodologies, and the like, when introduced without team members fully understanding what they do, are tools of force similar to saying "my way or the highway."

I once had a conversation with fellow product managers, and we were talking about the challenge of getting better real-time monitoring and testing from each of the development teams for their respective products in our production environment. One product manager mentioned that perhaps we should start using Test Driven Development (TDD). Some of the others nodded, but it quickly became evident that none of them really understood what TDD actually was. After describing TDD, it became clear that introducing it into the development cycle would have little overall effect in helping with our need, which was to get better real time testing and monitoring of our production sites.

TDD has a huge impact on the way developers work, and while developers learn this new process, velocity and time are lost. It may be beneficial, but the potential existed for dramatic disruption to our work effort by introducing a new process—all in hopes of addressing a problem that TDD wouldn't even fix.

The first step to resolving a problem is to understand why you have the problem to begin with. Apply the design principles of *Analysis* and *Decomposition* to your overall organization and composition of team members. Identify their fears and needs, and the real cause of your challenge should come to light. After this is understood, the choice of a process can be discussed in a manner that doesn't involve coercing, but does involve keeping the organization whole while still meeting the business needs.

If you don't understand why you are frustrated—then adding a process will not solve the problem. First, understand the principles of design, how it helps the process of change, then discuss adding processes to enhance and improve.

Force

We fear what we do not understand, and this is why it is so hard for us to embrace change. We often ignore our own fear, yet brand those who are unbending and do not want to change as a problem. Seeing problems in ourselves is the hardest.

A friend of mine shared a story to which helps to illustrate this point:

Jim was the oldest of several children, and liked to bow hunt. It was his time to get away and spend time time with nature. Each year his younger brothers begged to go with him, but he felt they were too small or not yet ready, or more honestly, they were too annoying. Then one year he finally relented and agreed to bring along the next oldest, Andrew.

Andrew was ecstatic, and prepared everything getting ready for the day, helping to pack the car the night before while doing his best to avoid being a problem to Jim. They drove into the mountains before dawn, and in the crisp pre-dawn air packed their gear and started crossing a meadow.

The first thing Jim noticed was how noisy Andrew was. It felt like he was going out of his way to step on every twig, stick and crinkled leaf. Trying to quell his growing frustration Jim stopped and whispered some terse instructions, "we need to be quiet. Watch where you step. Even the slightest noise will scare away the game!"

Andrew's eyes were big and he nodded to the instruction. They proceeded further, yet it did not change. Andrew was noisy, and all Jim could think about was how he would fail to get any game this year.

He shushed Andrew once more, yet it did not help. No matter how his brother tried, he was just too noisy. As they reached the far side of the meadow Jim finally lost his patience and turned to Andrew, "You are too noisy! Go back to the car, I'll be back later."

Tears welled up in Andrew's eyes. He didn't want to go back to the car, and he said, "but you are noisy too!"

Jim knew he was a good hunter, and he knew he was quieter than his brother. He shook his head and pointed to the car, flaring his eyes. Andrew retreated, his shoulders slumped.

As Jim continued into the woods, still stinging from the rebuttal Andrew had given, he noticed his steps. He wasn't as quiet as he thought. He too was stepping on twigs and making noise. But he had hunted so much alone, he had never noticed his own behavior, it had become edited out of his own awareness.

The focus on individuals being unbending and fearing change actually misdirects the conversation to the wrong place—the change itself. In this misdirection, the actual challenge—a person's needs—is trampled.

Most people who would normally be considered rigid and unbending are actually willing to accept change—once they understand the reason and need for the change, and once there is a plan in place that helps them to alleviate their fears.

---

66 *We often discuss change as a result of force.*

The plan is so important, to this step, yet is commonly skipped.

We often discuss change as a result of force. People who do not want to change are considered obstacles. But it is impossible to change anything that involves people by force. Each person involved must choose, of their own free will, to accept the change. If this is not done, that person is thrown into an emotional roller coaster cycle of ups and downs that draws parallels to the psychological phases of grief and mourning.

This becomes compounded for those who are dealing with things such as technology, where fear is so prevalent in the daily routine. If somebody tries to force a technological decision, they find the opposition as rigid as cold forged steel. Yet with proper communication, planning, and empathy, the would-be opposition may be as pliable as soft clay.

Thinking back to the statement that if a person does not wish to accept a change, then they can be introduced to the door. This is effectively saying: if they don't accept forced change, they will be fired. This statement, common as it may be, is toxic. Was the change communicated and managed properly by the very people suggesting to fire the individuals they are painting as obstacles?

There are some cases where a person simply refuses to embrace a change, no matter how much communication and empathy is used. However, in most cases where I have heard this declaration, it was an attempt to rationalize away the need and effort to properly plan and communicate a change and empathize with those impacted by it.

In a business world, this element of force amplifies fear, uncertainty, and doubt. If the culture of your workplace is, "do it this way or you can be reintroduced to the workforce," you are injecting a poisonous layer of fear into the entire effort. You may find a middling level of success, but any changes made in this manner are always less accepted and less successful than ones that come about when all parties are embraced and engaged.

Yet, if change can only happen by choice, what do we do with those people who do not want to change? They are commonly branded as obstacles, to be removed and overcome by any means, even dismissal.

The moment we look at a person as an obstacle, the person becomes an object, and there is no longer a relationship.

Instead, we need to ask ourselves: why are they resisting? At the root of the answer likely lies fear. The person is afraid of something, even if they cannot articulate the fear. Surprisingly, the answer may very well help the overall effort, if it can be discovered! It could be personal, such as the impact to them will be so great it will be detrimental to their ability to perform their job, or even to have a job. They could fear that their efforts to date would be wasted if the change is enacted, and this returns to the same fear conversation—why did they bother, and do they get to keep their job? Or perhaps they know their system well enough to realize the recommended change might be a problem for the business, and they are just not able to articulate the reason at that moment in time.

" *This person harbors fear because nobody has bothered to understand their needs*

This person harbors fear because nobody has bothered to understand their needs or even their customers' needs as they understand them—or at least they don't think anybody has. This is coupled with their perception that there is no plan in place to address these needs. Without a plan, the person assumes the worst: that these needs will not be met, their customers will suffer, and their ability to be a positive contributing member to the team, business, or workforce is now in jeopardy. When you feel resistance, it is on you to look inward and empathize.

Some argue that too much conversation can lead to a condition known as analysis paralysis, where the discussions seem to continue without end, and no decision is made. When the dialog is centered around the problem or even fixes to the problem, and not around finding the central fears and primitive needs (a need described at its most basic level), then analysis paralysis will abound. Any number of fixes can be made to a perceived problem, but until you speak to the fears that drive the problem, everybody involved will continue to feel unsatisfied. If you find the same issues are discussed over and over, then perhaps you have not yet found the base fears and needs.

The challenge faced is being able to empathize with those involved and helping them reconcile their fears and needs, so they—not you—will be the motivating factors to enact the change. This reconciling process sometimes can take time, but it can also be made in a focused manner. Each situation is different, and the elements proposed in this book are merely tools that may help in this process.

The core assertion is that, when somebody resists a change, it is most likely because you haven't done your job well enough for them to feel they are a part of the plan forward. To fix this, you have to have a plan and effectively communicate that plan. People cannot read your mind. Both of these efforts center on relationships and fear, not on how well you understand technology.

Sometimes a longer journey in making a plan is the best solution possible. I once encountered a situation where there were three competing technologies at a large corporation. All three had strong proponents and stakeholders. When the topic of consolidation came up, all three applications were proposed as being the best one to do the job, and all three had solid reasons.

The people behind each of the technologies each held an element of fear behind their reasons. What about all of the time and effort they had invested up to that point? Were they wrong to support the technology they backed? Would it reflect badly upon them if it wasn't selected? All of that aside, they each believed that the other tools could not meet their needs, and only the tool they had selected would do the job—after all, they had selected it.

The crusades were ready to begin.

The key stakeholders were engaged, but rather than discussing the technology features — or the requirements—we instead identified the core needs of the organization and the fears regarding the tool sets. Then we built a "Total Cost to Own" or TCO model around the business needs and operational framework. This led to a clear front runner selection, without ever getting stuck in the tar pit of technical capabilities against each tool. But even then there were holdouts—so the resulting plan involved a one-year reconciliation with the partner while they proved themselves by adding new features to meet our needs. By the end of the effort, most of those who were vehemently against the change were pushing for the consolidation, with a few singing praises.

Had the same effort come down as an edict, it is highly likely that there would still be three competing technologies in that organization, as the stakeholders behind each would find reason after reason for why they could not migrate. The plan succeeded because it was able to reconcile each person's fears and help them to know that the future change was predictable and safe.

Leadership Domains

Effective change can only be made with a solid understanding of your organization, and this involves understanding how people behave – these are defined as **Leadership Domains** and **Behavioral Domains**.

There are three common domains of leadership responsibility in a project: *Motivation, Vision,* and *Tracking*. These domains come with a variety of titles or roles, such as project manager, designer, architect, program manager, etc. Sometimes these domains are owned by one role, other times they may be distributed across a few. While one role may take point on a given effort, it is not at the exclusion of the other domain's input. All three domains must work together in empathy and understanding of each other's needs and fears.

Depending upon your organization, these domains may be grouped across individuals differently. However, if you consider them as three discrete domains, it helps to understand the primitive values provided by each domain.

The three domains are grouped in this manner because it divides the domains by common personality types and includes the contributions needed for successful execution of an effort. Those who are effective at the

Motivation role often struggle in Vision and Tracking. The same is true for grouping the other domains. There are always exceptions, and some individuals can handle two or even three domains with finesse. However, if your organization is sized to support it, these generally are best handled as discrete individuals who can work effectively together.

Spending time to understand where these domains and roles lie within your effort will help you to be successful in the Execution phase.

MOTIVATION

This domain holds the legitimate authority for the effort. The person filling this domain is the final decision maker, the person involved in motivating and guiding the other domains, and the primary leader for the effort.

VISION

Vision is the role of understanding the needs of the customers and building a plan that provides a path forward. This role is responsible for understanding the work efforts at large and providing a framework for the schedule, and is also the role covered by Architects. Those who best fill the role of Vision often have expertise and knowledge in the technology at play, which they can leverage as a base of influence in the matter, using Design Thinking principles.

TRACKING

Tracking is the role of accounting for tasks, schedules, and finances. Those who fill this role are great at budgets, tasking, scheduling, and "accounting" type work in the general sense of tracking information. It is taking the work effort at large and reconciling it to the available resources, schedules, and time, along with reporting progress in both work velocity and finances. Tracking is often completed by a Project Manager. Tracking takes lead on building project level documentation around process, contracts, and statements of work.

Behavioral Domains

Just as leadership has three common domains, the same goes for how people within an organization tend to think and behave. These are the Behavioral Domains and are commonly described as: **Operations**, **Engineering**, and **Architecture**. What varies is how each of these is defined within an organization. One group's engineering is another's architecture.

I suspect everybody has seen these described in a variety of ways, and there may not be a single best way to structure the separation of duties. The factors involved include how large your organization is and the focus of work effort. Larger organizations may have enough capacity to separate out operations and engineering duties, while smaller organizations may have to ask individuals to perform both domains.

With the improvement on operations technologies and the advancement of "Devops" concepts, the lines between teams are becoming more muddied, yet these domains remain relevant even within the a single team.

Coming to a consensus through definition of what these domains entail for you and your organization is valuable in reducing fears. I have found it useful to consider the aspect of time and how things are designed and implemented over time, when wrestling with this challenge (see *The Problem: Time*).

We have different people who have their own comfortable window of time, or basically have fixed upon a specific time frame of thought that works for them. Some of us will think on a scale of 1-3 months. These are the ER doctors who keep us alive on a daily basis. They provide life support when it is needed and are vital to our organization. But challenges lasting more than a couple of months do not concern these people, because their job is not long-term care, and they are just as apt to use duct tape and bailing wire to fix a problem as the proper surgical tools. It is immediate "get it done now" sort of thinking. These are the **Operations** people, often called fire fighters.

Others think on a scale of three months to half a year or so. These are the **Engineers** who could build a house in a week, if given the time to plan it out and the right amount of support. They figure out the tough details of making specific things work in the wild. They provide the glue and the bolts to make our infrastructure hum. But when faced with a challenge to build an infrastructure of interconnected skyscrapers, they might simply say the job is too complex and urge focusing on something they can get done in six months or less.

Architects bring in the long-game strategy. They think across all time ranges, from the next few months to several years. Sometimes called time travellers because they can think and often talk in all three time frames, the challenge of an Architect is to recognize the timeframe of their audience and focus the conversation to it. Instead of coming to the engineers and administrators with a multi-year conundrum of building an entire subdivision and talking about how to make it all work, the Architect should come to them with a one-month challenge, such as building the plumbing in a single house, and ask them to help make it happen.

"How to make it work?" you might ask. The idea seems so simple: just focus on the Behavioral Domain and put a label on it. The challenge is that people do not like to be pigeon-holed in such a simple manner. Everybody wants to do the design work for what they care about (be an Architect), yet keep focused on just their silo of effort for operations. Telling somebody that they cannot do design or architecture because they are now operations may very well be a recipe for disaster.

Design is an element that is most beneficial when it exists at all levels. If everybody should participate in the design process, then the leadership domain of Design is different from the general need for design across all behavioral domains—it becomes that of a facilitator to help others through the process of Design Thinking.

174

Project Management

We do not all have to be Project Managers. However, having an understanding of Project Management is a priceless skill and helps in clarifying relationships regardless of the position you hold. The first step comes in understanding what your organization expects from a Project Manager. This can fall to an individual only in the *Tracking* leadership domain, or to somebody who is both a *Motivation* and *Tracking* individual, or to somebody who just manages a portion of *Tracking* in schedules and tasks, but not finances.

Because the purpose of this book is not to repeat the breadth of information available on running a project, the following explanations are given only at a very high level.

There are a variety of project structures or process control models available to use, but generally speaking, there tend to be two types: *Defined* and *Empirical*. Defined is sometimes called a Waterfall process, where Empirical is conventionally considered an Agile process. Both types have their value, and understanding the full ramifications and impact of each is paramount to knowing what you are getting into.

Defined process control is one which defines early on and at a very detailed level how everything will be built. The complete architectural blueprint of a house, if you will. The deliverables are handed over in large chunks, if not all at the final deployment. This is how the world has managed projects in general, for quite some time. Yet it can be difficult to use in the technology industry, or any scenario where the process of figuring out what you want comes through the implementation—leading to a chicken and egg scenario: how can you define what you are going to build until you try to build it?

For the simplest explanation, consider "exploration" or "R&D" time. Every project manager in IT has faced the challenge of how to track this effort, where the technician cannot give a clear estimate of how long it will take to figure something out, let alone what steps are involved. But a defined process control mandates that they itemize the work items and how long each will take. However, the engineer doesn't know these things because the engineer hasn't done them before. Engineers are fearful in giving an estimate they cannot meet, and frustration abounds on both sides of the equation.

The challenge with a defined process in IT is that in many cases the details are simply not known at project initiation, and iterative phases of discovery are required as the effort is refined. If this is the situation faced, then the defined process may not be the best fit.

Empirical approaches have been developed to address this challenge. In technology, there is an unending need for exploration and refinement because the industry is constantly changing—but value also needs to be provided to the customer. With Empirical process control, the effort is divided into smaller deliverables, which can arrive more frequently. This approach's biggest challenge is a tendency to miss the strategic plan and matrix of needs, as the focus easily shifts to incremental delivery of the features a customer is asking for, instead of the strategic goal. If you find the conversations in Empirical planning are less about the long-term plan, or how needs are impacted, and are more about what features you can give a customer in the next iteration, you may have become derailed in your planning.

Both project structures can benefit from a well-designed plan. It is a common misunderstanding that an Empirical approach doesn't require a plan, and often any attempt to do longer-term planning in an Empirical process is disparaged as being 'too waterfall.' However, a plan is not the detailed blueprint and tasks required for execution, but rather a definition, at a high level, of the deliverables which a customer will receive and what needs these deliverables address.

Understanding this distinction is important.

Projects are commonly grouped into five phases: Initiation, Planning, Execution, Controlling, and Closing – although these phases tend to be considered with a Defined project model, these still exist even within Empirical projects. Design Thinking can play a role in each phase, regardless of the process control method.

During Initiation of a work effort, an idea is considered for its merit: do we create a project or not? Through architecture and a strategic plan, the organization has a perspective into the long-term direction, how this relates to the idea, and in what manner variances may need to be made.

Planning is the most important phase—as it is when the expectations are established as deliverables (regardless of how detailed they may be). Understanding *Decomposition* and *Analysis* is critical to make a proper plan that can be used as the blueprint for the rest of the project. The *Work Breakdown Structure (WBS)* is a valuable tool to use in documenting the deliverables.

Execution is typically defined as the start of the effort, where Controlling is the ongoing management and tracking of the project. Both phases use the defined deliverable to monitor progress and success. If using an Empirical effort, these deliverables can be used to reconcile that new sprints are staying on-track with what was defined, and that the proper order of deliverables is being worked.

Closing reconciles the final result of the project against the original designed blueprint to determine success, or if failure why the failure happened.

It is also important to recognize—in the context of conversational dissonance—that there are numerous assumptions bundled with each process control type. Because technology changes so rapidly, it has driven an industry in project management that is changing nearly as rapidly as the technology itself. People come from all sorts of places and have their own history. As such, they each have had their own exposure to different project management terms and processes, each implemented in its own unique manner.

Simply accepting an Agile methodology does not necessarily mean you are also accepting Kanban, Scrum, Extreme Programming, Continuous Integration, and the like. If time is not spent understanding and defining exactly the processes and methods you will use and making certain all team members are on the same plane of understanding, much confusion may result.

Becoming Effective

"To fix the mind is to foreordain the achievement."

- James Allen

The principles and ideas included herein are merely things I have identified as valuable. When I have remembered to apply these ideas, I have had great results. That isn't to say that I haven't made my own mistakes, as I'm sure my friends and colleagues are happy to remind me. The purpose in this writing is as much a reminder to myself as a benefit to any readers. I am confident there are many ways to address these challenges.

This book provides a variety of tools. Consider them like a buffet. Take the tools that are most important to you and your organization, and discuss them as a group. Once everybody has a common understanding of the principles that matter to your team, document them, and live by them as your Core Principles.

Applied Design Thinking

Empathize with the problem

- **Define** the problem by identifying the root needs. Seek the fears that are driving people before suggesting solutions.
- Strengthen your relationships during the process by **Researching** what others have done in the past, both successes and failures.

Take time to consider options **Creatively**

- Work with all teams to **Ideate** and discover powerful options. Don't let status quo bind your choices.
- Explore and **Prototype** options that address each party's fears.

Rationally approach resolving your need

* **Choose** the most powerful path forward.
* **Implement** it with a properly orchestrated plan. But be flexible, willing to change, make some mistakes, use frequent and effective communication, and have a defined mechanism to change the plan, when needs change over time.
* When finished, take time to look back and **Learn** from what went well and where you struggled.

APPENDIX-1

STRUCTURAL DOCUMENT

In this example you see the structural elements to a clustered nginx configuration with a failover VIP and loadbalancing an application cluster across two different availability zones.

Although a database is part of this solution, it is not included as the focus of this structural document is to discuss the failover capabilities of nginx, and unecessary details could make it more confusing.

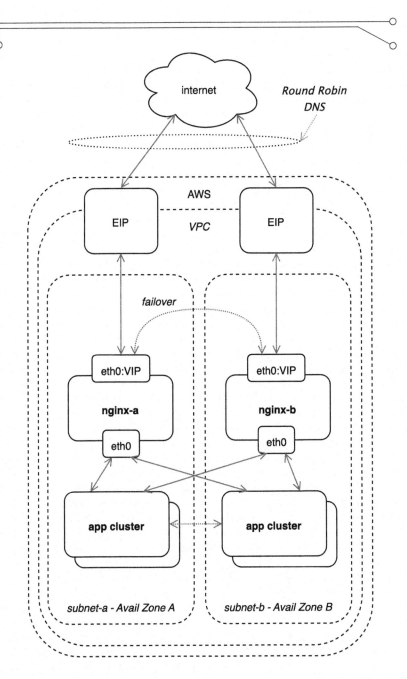

APPENDIX-2

BEHAVIORAL DOCUMENT

Contrasted with the structural document, this Behavioral document shows less of the networking and failover details (structural), and instead describes the flow of data including protocols used at different layers. Because the database is part of that flow, it also is shown.

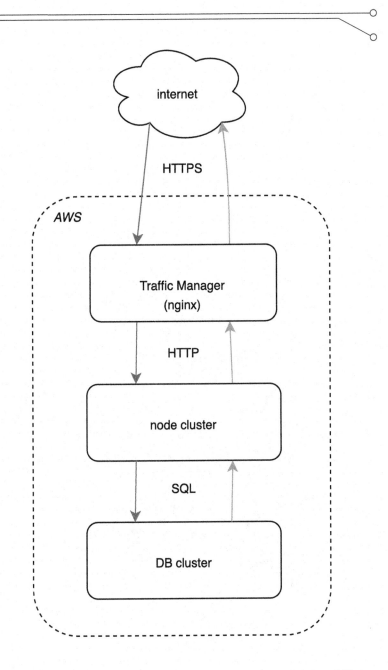

INDEX

Brandon has a breadth of experience, through his career including CTO, CIO, Director of Operations, Security and Infrastructure, Architect, Consultant, Engineer, Developer, and Project Manager across the public, private, and nonprofit sectors.

Some of his accomplishments include consolidating the Operational Intelligence strategy for a large organization with 1200 disparate systems; Architecting a large DoD compute facility and cloud stacks; defining policy used across the world for incident handling in a virtualized datacenter (RSA Conference and VMWorld presentations); and serving as Lead Architect on the team awarded Innovator of the Year from Red Hat.

As an entrepreneur, he has led the development of open source software with global team members, pioneered online game technologies, started several companies, and has developed for FreeBSD. More recently, he has created Reflex, an OSS tool to help with the modern challenges of ephemeral system/container management.

Brandon is a published author, loves all forms of technical or hacking topics, and blogs about them at http://surfingthe.cloud/.

Hailing from the slopes of Utah, he enjoys the outdoors with his family, tabletop games, and writing fiction.

CPSIA information can be obtained
at www.ICGtesting.com
Printed in the USA
FSOW04n0012100617
34951FS